IRISH LACE

MEMOIRS OF A MOTHER, GRANDMOTHER, AND PROFESSOR

PHYLLIS CAREY

Ten|16 PRESS

www.ten16press.com - Waukesha, WI

Irish Lace: Memoirs of a Mother, Grandmother, and Professor

ISBN 978-1-64538-030-6
Second Edition

Irish Lace: Memoirs of a Mother, Grandmother, and Professor
by Phyllis Carey

For information, please contact:

Ten|16
PRESS

www.ten16press.com
Waukesha, WI

Editor: Kaitlyn Hein
Cover designer: Tom Heffron

For our grandchildren and future grandchildren

Table of Contents

Introduction

Although I occasionally wrote short stories and poetry on the high school and college levels, I didn't really start to shape memoirs into narratives until the early 1990s when I was teaching an Advanced Composition course to college students, predominantly English majors. When the narrative assignment came up, I thought, why not? I'll write one myself, and as the class shared their stories and got feedback, I shared mine–the first version of "Chosen." The students offered good suggestions and seemed even more open to comments from me and their peers on their own writing.

After that, I found that when I shaped episodes in my life that had lodged in my memory into short narratives, the process helped me to find deeper meanings and on occasion the humor implicit in the human condition.

In 2006 when I retired from teaching, I had the unforeseen but in retrospect a truly blessed gift of caring for my then three-year-old grandson, Trent, who had recently been diagnosed with Type 1 diabetes and could not go to child care while his parents were at work or in college. The years 2006-2008 and the summers once Trent was in school became wonderful times for us to play, sing, create projects and just enjoy one another. When our own sons were young, I was teaching, and I seemed to be too busy to jot down what they said or what they did that was so cute, moving, funny, and/or insightful.

I also had the blessing of helping to care for my sister when she was dying of cancer in 2001, for my mother, who died in 2010 at 104 years old, and for my mother-in-law, who died in 2015 at 104 years old. These remarkable women gave me much more than I gave them.

My teaching experiences and chance encounters also provided much material for memories and notes. Students, colleagues, staff and administrators taught me much and helped me see the complex and sometimes comical patterns of language that emerge when we try to communicate with one another.

Over the years, I shared versions of the stories with colleagues, friends, and family. Their amusement and encouragement and their years-later, still-vivid memories of the accounts made me think there might be a more general audience for these writings. Although I have published scholarly articles and edited academic books, I hadn't considered putting out my private writings for the general public, but the response of family members, especially my husband, Pat, made me decide to move forward with the project. In the process of preparing the collection for publication, I updated some of the memoirs and scattered through them some of the tidbits I had collected from my childcare with Trent.

My Irish grandmother taught me to crochet, and in the course of sixty some years I have made numerous baby outfits, afghans, table runners, scarves, wall hangings, etc., mostly as gifts for special occasions. From my grandmothers and my mother especially, I learned to glimpse the threads that hold us together and to sense the intricate patterns that make up our lives. In the joys, frustrations, confusion, humor, sorrow and love I have experienced, I hope others will feel these complex and yet profound links.

Irish Lace

My grandma used to save the strands
Brushed from her long, graying hair
And lay them out in spring–
For wild canaries, robins, and wrens
Who gathered the slender threads
To knit and purl their nests.

My mother saved the delicate strands
Combed from simple, daily blessings
And wove them with the woes–
Through sorrow, grief, and loss
She drew fine threads of thankfulness
Into graceful shapes of hope.

I save the strands of memory
To stitch the stories of my life
Into patterns of sorrow and joy–
The wonder, the laughter, the tears–
Feeling through the fragile fibers
The spirit that holds us all.

Blessings in Disguise

Chosen

I read somewhere that the best subjects for writing are not those that the writer chooses, but rather those that *choose the writer.* Presumably, if there is something burning inside, writers will become more involved in the writing process than if they whimsically decide that a good topic might be the mating habits of wombats or which hand lotion has the best scent. In the 1990s, a subject was growing, gnawing, hounding me. There is no doubt in my mind that the topic—in my case—had chosen me.

On May 13, 1989, a *gift* arrived in Milwaukee by Air Express. The tag on the traveling kennel, like all baggage arriving at Mitchell Airport, had "MKE" in big letters. My then seven-year-old son assumed that "MKE" was its name, and the initials, pronounced "McKee," ended up as the family choice. Despite five years of obstinate refusal, I had finally, in a moment of incipient insanity, agreed that my brother-in-law could send a yellow Labrador puppy to our then nine and seven-year-old sons, Brian and Michael. After all, Uncle Jerry had sent Labs to all the Carey cousins, and both in-laws and dogs seemed content in the urban areas of Omaha, Rapid City, and

Saint Louis. Besides, growing up with a dog seemed to be one of those inalienable rights of children; it could be put off but had to be faced sooner or later. Parents could say *no* to pre-adolescent tattoos, pierced noses, and other bodily mutilations, but how many years could one say *no* to a cuddly puppy from a doting uncle? Since mine was the only dissenting vote in the family, I knew I couldn't hold out forever.

I could, however, I naively thought, protect myself. Since Labs make good yard pets, this *gift* need not interfere with my life. Voilà—the *pre-puppy agreement.* The night before the dog arrived, I whipped out a typed document listing my terms. I would take no responsibility for it. It would live in a dog house in the garage and not come into the house under any circumstances. The boys and their dad would feed it, water it, exercise it, bathe it, take it to the vet, groom it, de-flea it, and clean up after it. I would continue to enjoy my family and pursue my career without any interruptions from the new pet.

But rules that cannot be enforced are the *bête noires* of motherhood—or, in this case, the *bête yellow*. When we got the then small creature home from the airport and removed him from his cage, he was shaking and befouled with excrement and throw-up. I had no choice but to bathe him in the kitchen sink before the boys could play with him.

The animal then grew faster than the plant in *The Little Shop of Horrors.* By the time MKE was six months old, Michael wasn't strong enough to hold his leash, and Brian, who was strong enough, unfortunately had a weak stomach. Every time MKE did his business, Brian would try to scoop it up, only to regurgitate instantly. Who was going to scoop *that* up? When my husband, Pat, was away, I had no choice but to WALK THE DOG.

Four and a half years later, the sight had not become any less disgusting. Hovering around 100 pounds, the beast did not know the meaning of walking. His idea—or instinct—was to drag me down the street as fast as he could, stop abruptly to check his trees, spend the next five minutes sniffing with infinite care for every single blade of grass in a three-inch radius while grunting and slobbering copiously, then charge off at thirty miles an hour, yanking the leashed human behind him, pooper-scooper flying. The neighbors' jokes about one of my arms being longer than the other and about who was walking whom grew stale and faded—the truth could not be clearer.

Being towed by the dog, however, was the least of my problems. Unfortunately, MKE had a propensity to bark, which was natural but also maddening, particularly since his bark seemed at times to rattle the windows. Besides rubbing my nerves raw, the barking annoyed the neighbors. We received phone calls and hand-written notes from one neighbor complaining of MKE's barking, which she had distinguished from the barking of Spike, Ginger, and the other dozen dogs in the neighborhood. We tried everything, including a barking collar (which is decidedly not natural) to break him of the habit, but over the course of our efforts, we discovered an indisputable fact–except for a yelp when a stranger approached or another dog passed by, MKE howled incessantly only when I was around.

That's when I began disappearing. Since he lived in the back yard, I tried to hide so that he wouldn't think that I was in the house. I found myself whispering to my husband and the boys so that MKE couldn't hear my voice through an open window. On days when I arrived home first, instead of parking in the driveway and igniting a chain of barking that would last until the boys arrived, I parked up the street, tiptoed to the house, climbed over the porch railing, briefcase in hand, and silently slipped into the front door, hoping that the creature couldn't smell around corners and that the neighbors were not observing the spectacle.

Usually I was successful (with the dog at least), but the challenge came when I tried to fix dinner in the kitchen, where there were big windows without shades overlooking the back yard. Then I crouched in the shadows, like the woman in "The Yellow Wallpaper," slithering around the room, opening cabinets noiselessly. The woman in that story became obsessed with the wallpaper in her bedroom and ended up crawling in circles. She, of course, was mentally disturbed; I was simply trying to peel potatoes in a dark corner without arousing the yellow beast.

On days when I could not disappear, I tried other strategies. A dog with a bone in his mouth will not bark; ergo, bones. Lots of bones. Not the $5.95 jumbo basted rawhide, which MKE wolfed down in five minutes, but the 49-cents-a-pound soup bones I could pop into the microwave and toss out the window—like a gift from doggy-heaven. A well-chosen bone could give me a whole quarter hour of peace.

But the bones, of course, only intensified the problem. Every time MKE saw me, he seemed to see a bone, and the barking began. When he had already had his bone quota, I had no choice but to exercise him in the futile hope that he would become too tired to bark. Of course, the boys and their dad exercised him, but if he knew I was in the house alone, he would not stop barking until I was out in the back yard, running in circles, gasping for air, drenched in perspiration, while he stood, wagging his tail. As soon as I dragged myself back into the house, he was barking for more.

"Why didn't you take him to obedience school?" you may ask. Wait a minute, have you forgotten the pre-puppy agreement? This dog was not to interfere in my life. Was I supposed to give up an hour or two a week and practice obedience with him? Besides by the time he was three years old, when he already had me under his power, how was I going to wrestle control back? We both needed psychological help.

"Why didn't you get rid of him?" you may ask, also with good reason. I wanted desperately to send him back to Uncle Jerry as a "gift-in-kind." I found myself constantly composing letters—"Dear Jerry, an incredible thing has happened. It has been brought to our attention that according to city ordinance #426742, sec. XIII, part y, item 733—yellow Labs with inverted eyelids are prohibited within the city limits. It is very complicated, but we are making the best of it, and we are sure that MKE will be happy with you in South Dakota. P.S. I can't tell you all that having MKE has done to our lives."

I could have mentioned real city ordinances, of course, like the one prohibiting animals at large, particularly large animals at large. One afternoon as I turned the corner to come down our street—preparing to switch off the car motor and coast to a stop two houses from our own—I noticed clusters of neighbors standing on the block. As I rolled down the window to find out what was happening, one of the group called out, "Your dog is loose!"

I shifted mentally into emergency gear. Pat and the

boys were not yet home. What should I do? What *could* I do? I couldn't control the creature with a choke chain and a leash—how would I ever *catch* him? Then I saw MKE. He looked like a giant cougar as he emerged between houses and then became a yellow blur streaking up the block. I pulled quickly into our driveway, thinking that I should call 911. Visions of screaming police sirens and fire engines, however, quickly dispelled that idea. I thought of calling Pat, but it would take him fifteen minutes to get home, and MKE could have terrorized neighborhoods all the way to Delafield by then.

As I jumped out of the car, another neighbor four houses away pointed to her backyard where her own dog was encouraging MKE's attempts to break down the fence that separated them. The woman yelled, "Call your dog!"

Suddenly I glimpsed the widening gulf between me and normal humanity. The woman naturally assumed that if I called the dog, the problem would be solved. MKE would trot back home, and all would be well. I knew, however, without a trace of a doubt, that if MKE as much as heard my voice, I would be chasing him to South Dakota. For a fleeting moment, the thought occurred that this might not be a bad idea. I would call him, and he would run away—but that dog license on his collar would inevitably bring him back to us in one way or another. I gesticulated wildly to the neighbor, trying to convey to her wordlessly that calling MKE was the absolutely worst possible strategy, but the neighbor kept yelling, "Call your dog! Call your dog!"

There wasn't any time to spare. I thought of running in circles in the front yard on the chance that the dog would see me and at least come to watch, but the neighbors were already staring. It seemed as though I had been standing there for hours.

"Please, call your dog!" yelled the neighbor again.

I hurled my briefcase onto the front porch, jumped back into the car, threw it into reverse, and backed erratically up our one-way street to the neighbor's house. Then I opened the rear door, slid down in the driver's seat, and honked the horn. MKE liked to ride to the park with Pat and the boys—it was my only hope. I knew that the blaring horn from the seemingly driverless car was attracting even more neighbors, but I had run out of ideas. MKE finally stopped assaulting the neighbor's fence, looked around, then loped to the car and jumped in. I slammed the door, eased myself up only enough to see over the dashboard, and, ignoring the neighbors standing agape, I chauffeured the panting, slobbering Cerberus back to his own domain.

I realize, of course, that MKE didn't intend to humiliate me in front of all the neighbors, as animals don't have hidden agendas. No, he simply wanted me to show obeisance to his inflated sense of canine dignity, while systematically driving me into certifiable insanity.

On one occasion, he almost succeeded in achieving both goals simultaneously. Usually Pat or Brian put him to bed at night. One or the other went out, said "House!" and MKE jumped up from his favorite corner in the back yard and jogged into his doghouse in the garage. One evening with Pat and Brian at a late Brewers' game, the task fell to Michael and me.

Since the dog had a regular routine, I didn't anticipate any problems (but then for a well-educated woman, I am incredibly ignorant about animals, which, I am aware, is redundant at this point, but it's been a long time since I've had either the leisure or the luxury to concern myself with style). I went through the same ritual that Pat and Brian always performed, but when I said "House!" the dog simply sat down. He looked at me as if to say, "Commmme on, you have *got* to be joking! You must be the most deluded human on this planet if you think for one moment that I am going in that house."

I am convinced that I could move my refrigerator across the kitchen and back more easily than the effort it took to try to budge that beast. I tugged on one end, and Michael pushed on the other, but the animal might as well have been welded to the ground. On my suggestion, Michael threw pieces of cheese and salami into MKE's house, but the creature just sat there like a sphinx, staring at me with condescending triumph in his eyes. Finally, when Michael and I were both exhausted and I was about to succumb to primal screams, MKE stood up, shook himself off as though to remove any trace of our sweaty hands, and swaggered nonchalantly to the garage, into his own digs.

The next evening I announced at the supper table in my most dramatic voice that either the dog must go, or I would. The usual hum of dinner conversation stopped. There was a moment of silence. I glanced around the table and saw immediately that the choice wasn't as simple as I had expected. They loved MKE. He didn't bark constantly when they were around. He walked like a normal dog for Pat. He came when they called. Brian spent hours playing with him, visiting with him, and teaching him tricks. I had agreed to the dog. I had survived turtles, frogs, rabbits, fish and snakes. I would somehow survive this ordeal—although the ratio of one year of human life equaling seven years of dog life seemed much too generous to me—especially since I felt I was aging faster than the dog. Michael finally broke the silence: "Mom, is there any more spaghetti?" I decided not to call for a vote.

One September Saturday afternoon, I snuck out of the house for a stroll around the block to enjoy the late Indian summer sunshine. Two little neighbor boys were drawing pictures on the sidewalk in chalk. I stopped to admire their artwork and to chat for a few minutes. As I walked away, I heard one of the boys whisper to his friend, "That's MKE's mom."

"From the mouths of babes," indeed. Although I wasn't sure what lasting effects the dog would eventually have on my sons, the child's remark seemed to sum up, in all its implications, what had happened to me. I put the hand of my longer arm in my pocket, straightened my slumped shoulders and headed for home. Time to romp in the back yard before the three o'clock bone.

Addendum

At the time I wrote the previous narrative, I ended the story with the child's comment, but I had reason to add a postscript some time later, when the title seemed to take on a whole new meaning. Seven years later, I had more or less adjusted to being MKE's mom. As he aged, he seemed to have less energy to taunt me, and I gradually began to accept my fate. I usually took him for his morning walk after Pat and the boys left for school and before I headed out for the campus where I taught my afternoon classes. One day, however, is etched forever in my memory.

It was a typical spring garbage day. I had gotten the large green dumpster out on the curb and decided I might as well take MKE around the block for his morning poop before the garbage was picked up and before I disappeared. Normally, when MKE saw me pull out of the driveway, he knew it was futile to keep barking; he just waited until I tried to sneak back into the house. Of course, "normally" was never a word that fit in MKE's case.

As I hooked the leash on him, MKE tried to lick my hand as usual, probably his futile attempt to let me know he forgave me for being such a miserable pet owner. He had become less demanding with age but still seemed to think that our daily walk was an opportunity to show me he hadn't lost all his strength. I grabbed the pooper scooper as he dragged me toward the gate, and we were soon on our morning lurch. Sometimes I had to stand on the leash when I tried to pick up his leavings with the pooper scooper, to keep him from taking off for downtown Milwaukee, but this morning I managed to stretch the distance and grab it with the scooper claw without MKE's detaching my arm from its socket.

Signs of new life in the neighborhood brought that always welcome sense of spring. Bulging knobs on the tree twigs, green grass breaking through in patches, a robin on a low branch promised good things to come. For a brief instant, I almost felt glad I had a reason to go for a walk at 9:30 in the morning when everyone else was off to work, or at school, or engaged in some other useful activity.

I took the customary route, going around the block counter-clockwise. This day I was mentally checking garbage containers, spying an old soiled pillow emerging from a can and thinking it was time to get some new pillows for our beds. One neighbor had thrown out an old bike, and I wondered if it was salvageable for Goodwill. At one spot, an unclaimed pile of poop lay on the edge of the sidewalk, and I wondered if I should stop and pick it up as a mark of civic responsibility, But I quickly dismissed that thought on the remote possibility that if anyone in the seemingly-deserted neighborhood happened to be watching, my gesture might be misinterpreted as a sign of solidarity with dog owners. MKE tugged as usual, so I was also watching the uneven concrete to be sure I didn't trip.

We were approaching the corner of 58th and Elliott Circle when I happened to glance up. There, coming down the middle of 58th Street, just above the Circle, were two small shadowy figures in the bright morning sunlight. I couldn't make out clearly what they were at first, but as I stared, I realized that one of the figures was a small child, not more than two or three years old, skipping into the Circle street with a puppy that was about half his size trotting along ahead of him. Just as the reality of what I was seeing struck me, I heard and saw a garbage truck entering the one-way Circle half a block to my left.

I had no time to think. I ran into the Circle with MKE,

raised my free hand in front of the truck, and it came to a scrunching halt. I pointed at the child and puppy now approaching us in the arc of the circle and saw the look of alarm when the driver realized the situation as well. With MKE in tow, I ran to the child. I didn't want to frighten him, but I wanted to get him out of the street. I asked him if he was taking his doggy for a walk as I lifted him up with my free arm and brought him to the side of the road. He seemed unfazed by it all, as though it was the most natural thing that he was bouncing down the middle of the street and that I, a complete stranger, would come and scoop him up. Once we were all on the curb, the truck started up again, the driver shaking his head as though trying to bring himself out of the horror of the possibilities he had just faced and back to his daily routine.

As I juggled the child and MKE, who seemed to think the puppy trotting ahead of him down 58th Street might possibly be a new toy, I suddenly recognized the little boy. His family lived on 58th Street almost directly behind our house; he was the youngest of four boys. While I still held him in my arms, I told him I would take him home where his puppy was already heading. I don't know if canines have a sixth sense about these things, but MKE suddenly became a model dog, walking down the street on his leash, following the little dog, as though he was the puppy's parent or on display himself in a dog show.

I discovered, as I was ringing the doorbell of the house where the little boy lived, that I myself was in shock. How do you tell a parent that his child was walking in the middle of the street toward a truck coming around the Circle whose driver couldn't have seen him until it was too late? A drowsy father opened the door but immediately became alert at seeing his son in my arms.

"I guess your son decided to take the puppy for a walk. He was up on the Circle, walking in the street."

The father was visibly shaken. "I'm so sorry. I thought he was playing with his toys, and I dropped off to sleep in the rocker. He must have gotten out the back door." He gathered his son in his arms, and the boy snuggled in as though it was just a usual morning trip but good to be home again. The puppy crawled between my legs into the house with MKE giving him a quick lick.

MKE and I walked home, but I was still shaking. I got to the house and sat down with MKE, held his face in my hands and kissed him. He licked my face, and although his behavior didn't radically change after that, I felt we had reached a new understanding.

Some twenty years later, long after MKE had been put to sleep due to crippling arthritis, I encountered the little boy's parents at a university gathering. The father, now a middle-aged college theology professor, said to me, "I don't know if you remember that day so long ago when Nick went for a walk with the puppy. He was about three at the time, and you just happened to see him and got him out of the street. Every year I start my classes with that story. It's such a strong example of God's providence working in our lives in the most unpredictable ways, even when we ourselves are totally unaware."

No, I never forgot that day, nor the vision of those tiny shadows romping in a halo of sunlight. I realize, of course, that if MKE hadn't been taking me for a walk, the story might have had a very different ending. If he had made my life a bit uncomfortable—okay miserable at times—he was also tied to a larger mystery, chosen to be a vital thread in the fabric of a child's life.

Mother Wish

"I wish that Tommy was my brother."

The light of the birthday candles glowed on Brian's fair skin. His long lashes flickered a moment's shyness as though he himself had just heard what he had said. Tommy and Jonathan, his best friends, grinned at each other while Michael, his younger brother, seemed preoccupied with the cake.

"Hey, that candle's dripping all over the sport's pad!" Michael giggled.

Whether from the sight, or from Michael's comment, or from just the excitement of the moment, Brian, Tommy, and Jonathan exploded in mirth, inadvertently snuffing out two candles on the cake. It was my amateurish attempt to replicate a 1980s Nintendo sports pad—Brian's design—white frosting surrounding a grayish-green rectangle skewered with eight blue and red circles that looked like lurid eyes.

"Wait till the flash on the camera warms up," I said, impatient with my disposable camera and pondering Brian's unusual wish. I thought he would wish for the new bicycle he had been talking about for weeks, or a fish tank, or a fishing pole. I glanced at Pat, my husband, as I always did when either Brian or Michael said something with implications we thought they couldn't see. Pat's face had a bemused expression, but his eyes clouded for a moment, his eyebrows raised in a question as he glanced down on the tousled head of Michael, who was bent over the cake with Brian and Tommy and Jonathan. All four were now engrossed in restoring the missing flames for the traditional "make a wish and blow them out."

Brian's wish made me wonder, wasn't he happy enough with his own brother, with Michael? Was Michael's offering not enough? But then, Michael was not Brian's real brother, and we were not Brian's and Michael's real parents.

Then I remembered another wish a few years before when Pat was reading "A Doctor Talks to 5-7-Year Olds," and Brian in another unguarded moment offered, "Daddy, wouldn't it be great if I really was in Mamma's tummy?" A family friend had shrugged it off as a child's misunderstanding of anatomy, but Pat and I felt we knew what Brian was really wishing.

Now, in the shadows behind the giggling boys, I sensed a birth mother, remembering the lifeblood she had shed on this day eight years ago and perhaps wondering where her son was, perhaps even wishing for him. Like Michael's birth mother, she seemed always to be there, especially on birthdays, always there if frequently forgotten. On those occasions, the unknown fathers and mothers and perhaps blood or half-blood brothers and sisters seemed at times to take vague outlines and hover over the flesh-and-blood shoulders of our own family.

I thought of my own blood that would not nourish a child in my womb, no matter how great the hunger. Why won't it go away—this blood-wish—I asked myself.

And here was Tommy, with two blood brothers and a blood sister, shyly flattered by Brian's wishing, smiling his wide-toothed impish grin, chocolate milk crusting on his upper lip.

But, of course, Brian probably meant his words only as he seemed to say them as a sudden, passing thought—wishing his best friend could be even closer, wishing, for only a moment, that his affection for Tommy could reshape the facts. And, of course, it wasn't the first time that Brian came out with evocative questions or comments, but this one struck a chord.

The light on the disposable camera began to pulse its steady, reddish glow. Brian, gulping in air, braced to blow out the candles. And I wished the now time-worn, unattainable wish that he and Michael had been in my womb, blood of our blood, flesh of our flesh. The light flashed, the shutter clicked, the shadows shifted.

Two stray candles still flickered in red Nintendo eyes,

and Jonathan, in all innocence but betraying a tinge of hurt for not being the chosen one, abruptly reinforced the verdict:

"You won't get your wish anyway, Brian, because you told."

Weeks and seasons passed. The pictures of Brian's eighth birthday party sank lower in the stacked envelopes of snapshots waiting on the shelf to be sorted and filed away in albums. The boys' next birthdays came and went again with my customary nod to shadows and the dull ache of my own impossible wishing.

But like a time capsule in a sea of memories, my inner pictures of Brian's birthday journeyed on with me, drifting beneath the waves of daily routines, only to break the surface unexpectedly the day after I turned 50 years old.

How to celebrate my 50th birthday had been in the back of my mind since my 49th on January 16, 1990. Should I have a party, or should I let the date pass quietly and hope nobody noticed? My three older sisters and older brother had steered in two different lanes—two quietly letting the day slip by as they kept steady on the course of their lives, the other two pulling over to celebrate the landmark dates and the fact that they had each overcome so many roadblocks on the way. Pat marked his fiftieth by white-water rafting with the family on the Snake River in Wyoming.

The question of how to celebrate my birthday, however, dropped off my radar when on November 29, 1990, the UN Security Council announced the date of January 15, 1991, as the deadline for Iraq to withdraw from Kuwait. I couldn't believe the United States was actually contemplating going to war when the Cold War had just ended. Hadn't Communism crumbled in Eastern Europe without armies killing one another? Iraq invades Kuwait, so we invade Iraq. If invasion itself is wrong, how could our invasion be justified? Couldn't an unprecedented alliance of world leaders come up with a workable alternative to destruction and slaughter? Wasn't the blood running in the streets of Milwaukee and other major cities serving as clear evidence that the use of violence never solves conflict?

I wrote letters to President Bush, James Baker, and to our congressmen, arguing against the use of armed force in the Gulf. I talked with friends who supported a military solution, trying to understand how Hussein's pillaging and slaughtering in Kuwait could be fixed by our doing the same in Iraq. In December at a "Beyond War" awards ceremony, I saw a spokeswoman for Václav Havel dedicate the award to the children of Czechoslovakia—a profound gesture, I thought, since it is the children that fight the wars and suffer the most from the wars started by an older generation. In early January, I pondered late into the night the Congressional arguments for and against the use of military force.

On the morning of January 16, my 50th birthday, I was still convinced that one of the many last-ditch efforts for negotiation would be accepted. I had in-service meetings that day at the college where I taught, and I remember being struck by the irony of the situation as a spokeswoman for AT&T explained all the hi-tech components of our newly-installed phone system.

"Your new phone system will allow you to communicate in a number of different ways, wherever you are and whenever you wish."

I thought of the millions of people whose lives and whose futures hinged on whether two presidents decided to talk to each other.

Because I had been so preoccupied with the possibility of war, our plans for the evening had been made at the last moment; we would all go out for a quiet dinner to celebrate my birthday. As I came in the house from school, I heard Tom Brokaw's voice on the NBC nightly news. I sat down at the kitchen table, where Pat and the boys were waiting, to the flashes and rumbles of bombs bursting over Baghdad. As though a holding wall within me had crumbled, I began to weep. Through the blurred TV screen,

I sensed Iraqi mothers bending in dark closets and under sheds over their children, trying to protect them from the explosions and fire. Pat got up and mechanically began fixing sandwiches for the boys. His memories of telling parents their sons would not return from Vietnam in an earlier chapter of his life froze the features of his face. I went to our bedroom to grieve alone.

The next morning, Brian came by the open bathroom door while I was trying to mask the swollen lids of my eyes with blue eye shadow.

"Mom, yesterday was your birthday, and we didn't even have a cake!"

"I know, honey. It's just that with the war and all, I didn't feel like celebrating. But when this is all over, we'll celebrate, okay?"

"But Mom," he answered, "what if you're dead?"

I put down the mascara and studied his serious, frowning 10-year-old face. Hadn't we talked to him and Michael about the possibility of war? Hadn't we traced lines on the globe, showing them how far the Gulf was from us? Had the TV made him think that Iraq was nearby? Or was his anxiety coming from my own dread of war? Did he think it would last forever? Or was he simply worried that since Pat and I were older than the parents of most of his friends, we were in imminent danger of dying? What was going through his mind?

Before I could reply, his brown eyes lit up, and the words poured out, "I know, Mom!" he said. "If you can't blow out your own candles, I'll blow them out for you."

I grasped for some thread of logic in what he was saying. None of it seemed to make any sense to me. But his mention of candles suddenly parted the waves of my memory. I saw again his Nintendo birthday cake. I heard his birthday wish of two years before. I felt the pangs of my hungry wish.

Then an inner light flashed; a shutter clicked. I glimpsed for a moment the mystery behind Brian's statement. He had helped to fulfill my time-worn wish without even knowing it. We would never share a blood-bond, but I saw in his promising eyes the spirit-bond that will live on even after the earth has claimed my own flesh and blood. Brian's wish that Tommy was his brother and my long wishing that Brian and Michael were my sons by birth were essentially the same wish on some level, the desire for a concrete physical bond to witness to what we were feeling in our hearts. But for a moment I saw through the eyes of the heart that our love for each other was a sharing in a timeless, powerful human and divine love whose bonds transcend flesh and last beyond death. On the most enduring level, I *am* Brian's real mother. I *am* Michael's real mother. He and Michael could be no closer to me even if I had physically given them birth.

As I bent over to hug Brian, I thought of the mothers in Iraq, bending over their children, trying to shield their fledgling bodies and spirits from bullets and flames.

Addendum

Twenty-eight years later, Brian is now a thirty-eight-year-old adult, a plant engineer in a major cheese factory and a father of three wonderful children. He now has three additional special people in his life: Mel, Landen, and Kendra. Michael, a successful used-car sales manager, and his wife, Amber, are expecting their first child. Michael and Brian are not only brothers but best friends. Now a grateful, proud grandmother, I fear the world our children and grandchildren face, a world of our own making.

Since the Gulf War in 1991, we as a nation have experienced 9/11, the war in Afghanistan, the Iraq war, and the war on ISIS. In addition, since 1990, we have witnessed mass shootings at Columbine, Orlando, Sandy Hook, Fort Hood, Virginia Tech, Las Vegas, Parkland, just to mention the more well-known. Hundreds of thousands killed, wounded, maimed, scarred for life. The separation of mothers from their children at our southern border, as though they were animals, is one of the latest and most dehumanizing actions outside of war the United States has ever practiced and condoned. When tangible family bonds mean nothing, where do we find hope for humanity? As a nation and a world, we seem to have become even more divided, angry, and suspicious of one another. We contemplate building concrete and legal walls. We exile people who have been productive citizens in our country and ignore the agony of refugees fleeing violence. We seem to have become more and more numb to the violence and brutality in the daily news.

My "mother wish" was transformed on that day in 1991, when my son helped me glimpse through the eyes of the heart that our family was connected by human and spiritual bonds that can be even stronger than the bonds of blood relatives. My prayer now, my "grandmother wish" as an aging senior, is that we can begin to see through the darkness and brutality of this physical world the invisible threads that link us all as brothers and sisters, mothers and fathers, daughters and sons in the human family.

Sweet Dreams

"G'night, honey."

"G'night, Grandma."

"God bless you."

"God bless you."

Thus began our usual bedtime litany while I was tucking in our then three-year old grandson, Trent, who often stayed overnight with us.

"Don't let the bed bugs bite."

"Don't let the bed bugs bite."

"Sweet dreams."

"Sweet dreams." A pause. "Grandma, what dream do you have?"

Without thinking, I told him about the recurring dream I had been having of driving up a steep hill and not being sure if I would make it, clearly in my mind symbolic of the anxiety I was experiencing. I didn't interpret the dream for him, though. I just described in a matter-of-fact, detailed way the car, the hills, the obstacles that popped up and my attempts at driving, hoping his eyelids would grow heavier.

Instead, he responded, "I hope I have the tomato dream."

"What's the tomato dream?"

"I dream I'm in a giant tomato—it's all soft and mushy, and I have a big spoon, and I eat and eat the tomato, and I don't have to have my blood sugars or my shots or anything! And I have a great big tummy, and I fall asleep in the tomato."

"That's a beautiful dream, Trent."

A few days after our bedtime dream conversation, Trent was sitting on my lap while I was checking out the blizzard forecast on the computer.

"Look, Grandma! There's your dream!" he said, pointing at a box on the weather site with a blue car at an impossible angle struggling to climb a hill. It was the Weather Channel Driving Game. We clicked the box, and Trent was off, driving the blue car through a maze of slippery roads, steep hills, and rain, with rocks, trucks, and blue-and-yellow Weather Channel umbrellas looming up in the middle of the road. "Grandma's dream" quickly became his favorite computer game. One day when he finished the game with the car safely "home" and bonus points for hitting the umbrellas along the way, he turned to me and said, "See, Grandma, it's not so scary!"

Trent was diagnosed with Type 1 diabetes in June 2006. He had his third birthday only two months earlier and had shown few symptoms except an increasing thirst and the need to urinate often. Since he was potty training at the time and enjoying the control he was gaining over his body, and since the weather was warm and he was very active, the symptoms were chalked up to all of those other factors until he started to go into shock from his elevated blood sugar and was rushed to the hospital where he was diagnosed. He stayed in the hospital for four days, adjusting to a new life of four shots of insulin and at least four blood sugar tests a day.

Lesson learned: Unusual thirst and frequent urination in small children can be a sign of something serious. Even if there is no family history of diabetes, get the symptoms checked out.

Children tend to be resilient, even with terrible diseases. Trent seemed to adjust to his diet and regimen of blood sugar tests and shots within a matter of weeks. Bright and articulate for a three-year old, he would correct me when he was staying with us if I inserted the lancet "the wrong way," failed to produce the necessary drop of blood, or deviated in any other way from his usual routine.

One day when Kim, his mom, came to pick him up, saying she would give Trent his lunch shot, I had a moment of silent but significant recognition, an "epiphany" as it were, in literary terms. I realized that I was greatly relieved not to be giving the shot, that I had been dreading the finger pricks and the shots. I had even been counting how many shots I would be responsible for giving when Trent came for a few days. I also realized that I had been over-reacting to normal everyday ups and downs. The night before, Trent had come in with his Grandpa and said, "I'm tired," and I immediately switched to emergency mode until Grandpa, seeing my facial expression, said, "No, he's just tired. We've been working hard playing golf out there." I also remembered that Trent increasingly had been saying "I'm not hungry" when it was time for blood sugars and meals, possibly thinking he could avoid the blood sugars and shots but also maybe unconsciously protecting me from giving them.

Lesson to learn and relearn: Children pick up the fears and anxieties of those who care for them; they do not need the extra burden of worrying about caretakers who are anxious about their illnesses.

From that moment on, I began trying consciously to put Trent's diabetes into a different perspective. I concentrated on seeing my wonderful grandson again, who is extremely gifted and happens to have diabetes, rather than seeing everything primarily through the lens of diabetes. Although I still had concerns, I felt a burden had been lifted. I no longer counted how many shots I would be responsible for. The shots and blood sugars faded into routine, rather than looming as moments of dread. And Trent didn't say he was not hungry nearly as often as before. *See, Grandma, it's not so scary.*

After Trent told me his tomato dream in March, we got him a "Buzzy: My First Tomato Kit" for his fourth birthday on April 1, 2007. He and Grandpa planted the seeds, and after two transplants, he had 65 plants and the promise of a rich harvest of tomatoes.

A few weeks later at the supper table, Trent asked, "Grandma, will I always have diabetes?"

Before I could answer, he said, "Mom says it doesn't go away. I think I will die from diabetes."

"Trent," I said. "Remember your tomato dream? Do you want to know what my best dream is? I am dreaming and hoping and praying that a cure for diabetes will come not too long from now and that someday you won't have diabetes any more. In the meantime, though, you can still eat all the tomatoes you want."

I wonder about the wisdom of building up hopes for something that may not happen, but then I am reminded of all the progress that has been made in treating diabetes in the last few decades. I'm also convinced that rather than passing on fears and anxiety, it is far better to nurture hope. And, of course, the tomato dream, with all its hope, was Trent's dream to begin with.

At least eight people, including Trent's great-grandmother in Iowa, received potted tomato plants from the seeds he planted, and the rest were planted in our garden. Finally, after numerous meals with tomatoes, eighteen frozen cartons of tomato sauce and over two dozen containers of salsa—all from the seeds of one Buzzy tomato kit—"Trent's tomatoes," as they were known in the family, were all harvested. Trent and Grandpa had their picture in the local paper, smiling over the huge tomato harvest. Surprisingly, two potted plants, one in Iowa and one in Suamico, Wisconsin, with Great Grandma Knight and Grandma Magyar, were still producing tomatoes in late October. Trent munched on his own tomatoes for six weeks and had lots of spaghetti sauce over the winter.

Lesson learned: A dream can grow in many ways, and even if we don't know if that dream will ever come true, it can continue to nourish us every day.

Wishing Well

Our grandson Trent was four, and he and I were at Walmart, inspecting the spiral wishing well with the coin funnel. I relayed to Trent the directions, "It says, when you put the coins in to see where they go, you should make a wish. Do you have a wish?"

Trent: "I wish Grandpa's back would feel better."

Me: "What a nice wish, Trent! You must tell Grandpa that."

Later, at lunch time at home, I said to Trent, "I wish you would eat your applesauce."

Trent: "Grandma, you have to put money in the magic well and make the wish, and maybe tomorrow it will come true."

The next day, having already forgotten the key to success, I said, "Trent, I wish you would eat your banana."

Trent: "Grandma, remember the magic well?"

Me: "Yes, but that was yesterday, and I wished you would eat your apple sauce, but now I want you to eat your banana."

Trent smiled, "No, I'll eat the applesauce. That's how magic wells work."

Expanding Consciousness

Nature's Poetry

From the time he could walk and talk, our grandson Trent has loved to be outside. He loves the birds, the plants, the animals, even the bugs, and he made me much more aware of them when we were together. In the car one time when Trent was three, we were listening to "The ants go marching two by two," etc. and the lyrics said, "The little one stopped to ride a bee." I asked how anyone could ride a bee, and Trent replied, "Grandma, it's an ant. An ant can ride a bee. The song is about ants, not people!"

We were out taking pictures of the new sunroom one day, and Trent, with his toy camera, said, "Wait, Grandma, I want to take some pictures of those bugs." There were bugs flying over my head, so I fluffed up my hair and said, "Okay, does my hair look all right? Do you want me in the picture?" "No," he said, "I just want the bugs."

Trent especially loved birds when he was a toddler. One night when he was kissing me goodnight, he pursed his lips so he had a squeaky sound. "Grandma," he said, "that means there is a little birdie inside you. It's nice and warm, and it has a warm nest, and it's singing in there."

Another time, en route to Kindermusick, Trent asked,

"Grandma, how come the birds don't get zapped when they sit on the telephone lines?" I thought about it for a minute but couldn't think of a reasonable explanation. Trent said he bet his dad would know, so we called Brian, and Trent asked the question. When the conversation was finished, Trent said, "Grandma, it's because the birds are grounded. Isn't that great, Grandma? The birds up in the air on the wires don't get zapped because they're *grounded!*"

Instead of throwing away old bread, crackers, chips, etc., I saved them and threw them on the beach for the seagulls, geese, and small birds that were looking for snacks. Trent and I often went down to the beach "to feed the birds." Once, Trent poured out the old bread and then decided to pick up twigs to make a little wood pile in case the birds wanted to cook out. Then he threw twigs and branches into the lake so the birds could sit on them when they wanted to fish. He was sure that with the bread, the twigs for a bonfire, and the branches for fishing, the birds could camp out and have a great time.

Trent has loved projects since he was a tot, and the projects were frequently related to birds in some way. I usually planned things we could make when he came, and he got into the habit of asking what project we would make on a given day: papier-mâché animals, baking cup flowers, puppets, bird feeders, painted rocks, paper airplanes, cardboard cars, cookies, dream catchers with bird feathers.

In the summer of 2009, when Trent was six, we decided to make a special kind of bird feeder. We usually just used peanut butter on paper rolls and rolled them in bird seed, but this time, we bought a huge block of suet at Newton Meats and then cut off some slabs to melt down and use for bird feeders we had seen on the Internet. You take cans and fill them with the melted suet and when the suet has dried, you roll the suet in bird seeds and then put them in cans until they harden. After we did all that, we went to pull the bird feeders out of the cans with the strings we had embedded, but as we were trying to pull them out of the cans, the bird feeders all disintegrated. It was clear that we had used too many seeds and not enough suet. Although disappointed, of course, I thought this was a teachable moment for Trent, so, thinking he would figure out that we needed more suet as glue, I asked, " Now what did we learn from the way these feeders all fell apart?"

Trent answered without hesitation, "Never make this project again!"

Besides birds, as a young boy, Trent loved gardening and plants. His great grandmother, Doris, is a master gardener. Because of her influence, Trent at a young age became a miniature gardener and naturalist. He loved plants, bugs, and worms, and he sometimes sounded like Grandma Doris. One day we were walking around the garden, and he said, "That's a weed in Grandpa's flowers. We'll have to tell him about that." He pointed out gypsy moths, crickets, and grasshoppers, and often talked to them as he was walking or riding his bike. An unusual plant was growing in one of the planters, and Trent said, "Looks to me like a pumpkin plant." Another time, Grandpa was pulling weeds, and Trent stopped him as he was about to pull a particular one and yelled, "No, Grandpa, that's an azalea!"

In the spring of 2008, when Trent was turning five, we were having a particularly bad time with baby moths. One day there was a baby moth on the kitchen wall. Trent asked what moths do, and I told him they liked to eat holes in material. Grandpa was wearing a thirty-year-old Irish sweater, and it had a few holes in it, so when Trent noticed them, he said, "Grandpa, the moth ate more holes in your sweater!" Trent tried to catch the moth with a jar to put it outside, but it got away, and we couldn't find it. I asked him where he thought it went, and he said, "It's probably upstairs eating up all the blankets and clothes."

One school break when Trent was seven, I took him to the John Michael Kohler Museum in Sheboygan. Among other displays, we saw a nature display with lots of animal pictures, statues, etc. made by children. The next day, Trent and Pat glued together a bear made of pine cones that Trent had collected at Grandma Doris' house. When it was done, Trent asked me if we could take it to the museum to put on display. I told him I wasn't sure about that, but he said that if we did, he would put a sign on it that said "Made by an 8-year-old."

"But you're seven," I said.

"I know, Grandma, but no one would ever believe a seven-year-old could make this bear."

Making Meaning

Learning language is one of the wonderful things children do as they grow, but it can be confusing and even troubling at times. Trent and I were leaving the supermarket one day when he was three, and I was loading the car with our groceries when some neighbors came by and greeted me. I said "hello" to them, and Trent asked, "Who is that?" I told him it was "just some neighbors." Without any warning, Trent started to cry, "But Grandma, I'm your neighbor. I want to be your neighbor." I gave him a hug and asked him why he was crying. He said it was because I could only have one neighbor, and he was my neighbor. I tried to explain to him what "neighbors" are, but then it dawned on me that he was thinking of Mr. Rogers' song that I often sang to him, "It's a beautiful day in the neighborhood, a beautiful day for a neighbor, would you be mine? Could you be mine?. . ." I gave him lots of examples of neighbors and reassured him that he was not just my neighbor as in the song, but my grandson, and that he couldn't be more special to me.

Three going on four, Trent was at that age when he began to draw a picture or write something, and when I asked him what it was, he said, "I won't know until it's finished." Then when he was done, he asked me what it was.

When he was four, he began printing letters, and then taped his creations on the kitchen counter. One of them was "TAREDODODE." When he showed his dad, he said, "See, I wrote ta-re-do-do-de." When Brian asked him what it meant, Trent looked at his dad like he was illiterate and said, "It means ta-re-do-do-de."

Another time he wrote a long line on a sheet of paper, handed it to me, and said, "What does it say, Grandma?" When I said I couldn't read it, he replied, "It says you should go to the grocery store and buy lots of good food for Trent."

Helping children expand their vocabulary is always a challenging but fun time for adults in their lives. Sometimes, they surprise you.

Trent, age 4: "Grandma, what's that in the picture?"

Me: "It's something doctors use to hear how your heart is beating."

Trent: "Oh, I see! It's a stethoscope!"

Sometimes, children come up with their own descriptions, which are often more creative than the technical terms. While our sunroom was being built, we would hear occasional snaps and cracks. Trent asked, "Grandma, what's that noise?" I told him that the windows and wood were expanding and contracting, and assuming he wouldn't know those words, I was about to explain, when he said, "Oh, I know, Grandma. They're getting comfy!"

Of course, sometimes children pick up vocabulary that gets a bit mixed up in their minds. When he was four, we saw some little "magic wheels" in a store, and I asked Trent if he would like one.

Trent: "Do they come with destructions?"

Me: "I think you mean 'instructions,' but 'destructions' is probably a better word."Another time, when Trent was six, his mom called to say that he had been riding his scooter that morning and came running into the house shouting, "Mom, the scooter has Grandpa's name on it! Come and see." Kim went out of the house with him and looked where Trent was pointing.

"See, Pat 64598!"

Kim explained "patents" to him and told him that although his grandfather's name was "Pat," the number wasn't a reference to him.

Trent responded with, "Mom, do you think Grandpa owns all the scooters in the world?"

After I picked Trent up for the day when we came to Exit 144 on the highway, I sometimes would say, "Here's our exit!" One day when he was four, Trent corrected me.

"Grandma, it's 'ex-it'; say it after me, 'ex-it.'"

"'Ex-it.' Isn't that what I always say?"

"No, Grandma, you say 'eggzit' not 'ex-it,' and every time you say it, I think of those big fluffy eggs with the soft centers, and sometimes they have salsa sauce to go with them, and sometimes there's cheese on top. Do you know what eggs I'm talking about, Grandma?"

"I think so."

"I'm hungry, Grandma."

One time when Trent was in second grade, I stopped for gas, and when I got back in the car, Trent said, "It's really windy." I replied, "Yes it is, but it's windier in Green Bay." Trent answered, "Grandma, it's '*more windy*,' not '*windier*.' I looked it up when I got home, and apparently, both are right; it reminded me of the "*exit*" experience.

Of course, vocabulary is one thing, and human anatomy is another. Children don't always understand how the human body functions. I still remember when four-year-old Trent asked me, "Grandma, when you were a little boy did you have jets in the tub?"

Grandma: "Trent, I never was a little boy."

PAUSE

Trent: "Did you just come out that big?"

Another time, I asked four-year-old Trent if his cold was keeping him awake at night. "No, Grandma," he responded, "I don't breathe while I'm sleeping."

One day when he was eating his lunch, Trent said he was full and was ready for dessert, but he still had a plate with a half-finished sandwich, apple slices and carrots. I asked, "How can you eat dessert when you're full?"

Trent replied: "That's just my lunch tummy. My dessert

tummy is empty."

Sometimes his own questions were perfectly logical, but unintentionally embarrassing. One time I took Trent to his swimming lesson, and, as usual, he wore his swimming suit under his clothes. Unfortunately, I forgot to put underwear in his backpack, so after swimming, he had to put on his clothes without his underwear. Later, we stopped at the library, and a middle-aged man held the door for us. In the process, Trent stopped, looked up at me and asked, "Grandma, why did you forget underwear?" The man looked at me and winked. I thought I was too old to blush but found out differently that day.

Another time I was at Walmart and called Kim, Trent's mom, to check on his size. Trent was home and wanted to talk to me, and when we were finished, he said he was sending me a kiss and a hug. We frequently exchanged kisses and hugs that way in person, especially when either one of us had a cold. I told him I was sending back kisses and hugs. I always exaggerate the sounds and asked him if he got them. I didn't realize until I looked up that a few people were watching and apparently wondering what kind of conversation I was having.

At times, Trent amazed me both by his growing vocabulary and his thoughtfulness. When he was just turning seven, he came for Easter and stayed overnight on Sunday and Monday. I had dyed Easter eggs, and he had some for snacks. On Sunday night, Pat said he would like to eat an Easter egg, too, so I told Trent to take one into Grandpa, but he took the whole egg carton where I was keeping the painted eggs. When he returned, I asked, "Why didn't you just pick an egg and take it into Grandpa instead of taking the whole carton?" Trent replied, "Grandma, Grandpa has to pick the egg he wants. I couldn't just pick out one randomly to give to him. I might have picked a green, and he wanted a yellow." I was amazed that a budding seven-year-old could use the word "randomly" correctly.

Another area of expanding consciousness was in the changing dynamics of the family. When Alexander Brian was born Sept. 15, 2009, to Brian and his second wife, Justine, Brian called us and asked to talk to 6-year-old Trent, who was staying with us at the time. Brian wanted to tell Trent about his new little brother. Trent then asked him what the baby's name was. When Brian told him, Trent said, "Oh Dad, you should have called him Trent 2!"

When Trent was eight, Kim, his mom, and Brent, her second husband, were expecting a baby. When Kim told Trent that she was going to have a baby, he said "Great! I'll have a baby brother at my dad's and at my mom's!" Kim told him that it might be a girl, and Trent asked, "Can't you put her back in until she becomes a boy?" The baby turned out to be Benjamin, so Trent ended up with a baby brother at his dad's and one at his mom's.

Grandpa Stories

When Trent was first diagnosed with diabetes and getting four shots a day and at least four needle pricks at age three, sometimes he would cry when a shot or needle prick hurt. Grandpa would try to distract him and say, "Didn't hurt me!" Trent would laugh, but then came to expect Grandpa to say it. As soon as he started to cry, I would say, "What's Grandpa going to say?" and Trent would say, "Don't say it! Don't say it!"

One day, when Trent was four, we stopped at a service station to get gas and pick up some bread, and when the girl at the counter stood up to wait on us, she hit her head on an open door of an upper cabinet. She was clearly in pain, and while I was commiserating with her, Trent piped up, "You know what my grandpa says?" I said, "Don't say it! Don't say it." But Trent, smiling, couldn't resist, "Didn't hurt me!" I think the girl thought Trent was an insensitive brat, but nothing could be further from the truth.

The saying has become part of the family culture. A few years later when we were flying kites, I twisted my ankle and fell. While I was trying to assess if I really sprained it or just pulled a muscle, Trent, trying to console me, I think, but also perhaps sensitive to my pain and afraid to be too direct, offered, "Grandma, remember what Grandpa always says—'Didn't hurt Grandpa!'"

Of course, repeating what Grandpa said was one of Trent's early habits. One day when he was four, Trent, Grandpa, and I walked over to a neighbor's house, and when we were coming back, the trash that the wind had delivered by the front barn at the beginning of our long driveway was unsightly. Snow had melted, and there was a big piece of cardboard and a wind socket that looked like a clown. I picked them up to bring them back to our trash cans and suggested as we walked down the driveway, "This wind socket isn't in that bad of a shape. We could hang it up somewhere." Pat responded, "Burn the damn thing." The next day when Kim came to pick up Trent, the wind socket was on our front porch, and I asked her if she wanted it. She didn't think she would take it, but then Trent chimed in, "'Burn the damn thing.' That's what Grandpa said. 'Burn the damn thing.'"

Of course, Trent didn't always approve of everything Grandpa said.

Trent: "Grandma, Grandpa called you 'Old Grandma,'" but I don't think you're old. You're not even 100! So why does Grandpa call you 'old,' Grandma?"

Me: "Trent, I think Grandpa is just kidding."

So Trent went back to Grandpa:

Trent: "Grandpa, when you call Grandma 'Old Grandma' you're kidding, right?"

Grandpa: "Yes, I guess so."

Trent: "You know Grandpa, kidding is lying, and you're not supposed to tell a lie."

Grandpa: "How do you know that?"

Trent: "That's the rule. You don't tell lies." And then after a short pause, "Grandpa, I think you need a time-out."

Of course, Trent became aware of some nuances of language. After lunch one day when he was six and had spent a lot of time playing outside, Grandpa said that Trent should probably take a nap. Trent said "Yeah, right." Then he said to Pat, "Grandpa, you know that 'Yeah, right' means 'probably not.'"

"I can't believe" was one of Trent's introductions that sometimes was very funny. One day during potty training, after having a bowel movement, he said, "I can't believe I can wipe my own butt!" I replied, "Yes, honey, I think that's marvelous." Trent asked Pat, "Grandpa, do you think it's marve'lous that I can wipe my butt myself?" Pat responded, "Yes, that really is marvelous." Trent asked, "What does 'marve'lous' mean?"

Usually Grandpa took Trent to bed while I finished up dishes or the laundry, but although he loved sitting on Grandpa's lap and doing all kinds of projects with Grandpa, for some reason, Trent really liked it when I took him up to bed. One Sunday night during March Madness, Trent came into the living room and asked Grandpa, who was watching basketball at the time, if he could change the channel to watch cartoons. Grandpa let him change the channels (only Trent would suggest such a thing to a sports' addict, and only Trent asking for it would move Grandpa to change channels). Not much later, it was time for bed, and I told Trent that Grandpa would take him up.

Trent asked, "Grandpa, don't you want to stay down here and watch basketball?" Grandpa laughed and said, no, that he was tired and would take him up. Trent sighed and said, "I knew I shouldn't have switched that channel!"

Another time when they were up in bed, Trent said, "Grandpa, couldn't you do the dishes and clean up the kitchen so Grandma could put me to bed?"

One time I did take him to bed when Grandpa was watching a particularly important basketball game. When Trent was all nestled in his bed, he said, "I just can't believe how lucky I am to have Grandma put me to bed!"

When Trent was five, Grandpa did some lecturing in China. On the weekend when Trent stayed overnight, he noticed both cars in the garage. He asked, "Didn't Grandpa drive a car to China?" I said, "No he flew." Trent said, "Oh, when I saw the two cars, I thought maybe you just dropped him off."

There was a hornet in the house that afternoon, and

Trent thought we should call Grandpa in China. I said that China was too far away for Grandpa to come to help, but Trent said he didn't need to come to help, he could just tell us what to do over the phone. Later that night, Trent said he was scared. When I asked him why, he said, "Grandpa gets rid of the monsters, but Grandpa isn't here."

One day when Trent was six, and we were driving into town with a full schedule ahead of us, I ran down the items on our agenda. "First, Post Office, then Kindermusik, then the grocery store, then the bank, then home, then lunch, then snooze." And I stopped, but Trent picked up, "Then mow with Grandpa, then happy hour . . ." Late in the afternoon, Pat usually says "Time for Happy Hour!" and Trent is with him in spirit, if not spirits!

The Joys of Technology

Growing up in Technocracy

When I was a child in the late 40s and early 50s, I was only vaguely aware of the changes in technology that were gathering momentum and would begin to overwhelm us in the 80s, 90s, and 2000s. As a child, I had to give the operator our telephone number, and I knew that at times she listened in on our calls. We listened to the radio at night—the first television sets, in black and white, were miracles.

Of course, by the time our own children were growing up in the 80s and 90s, times had changed considerably. I remember putting our son Brian (Trent's dad) to bed one night when he was just four. He looked up at me and asked, "Mom, does God turn the sun off at night so the batteries won't run down?"

It wasn't until I babysat Trent, however, that I became aware of how much current technology has pervaded the lives of infants, toddlers, and preschoolers. Not to mention the lives of all the rest of us. For one thing, the vocabulary of the computer is part of their everyday language. On the way to music one day, I told 4-year-old Trent to remind me to read a birthday e-mail to him when we got back.

When I asked him if he would remember to remind me, he put his finger on his forehead and said, "Just a minute–*enter*." Another time, Trent and I were racing to see who could get their pajamas on first. I was in the closet and he was in the bathroom. He was having trouble getting his top on and yelled at me, "Grandma, can you push *pause* for a moment?"

Of course, children adapt more easily to devices when they are young than we older people do. When a CD came that I wanted Trent to hear, I tried to get it going but to no avail. Trent was having lunch with Grandpa, and I heard him say, "I suppose I'll have to go get it running for her." He came in the other room and showed me what buttons to push.

And of course, the computer has all the answers. One time, when he was coloring, Trent used the word *Arriba*. He said it was on one of his cartoons, "*Arriba*! *Arrib*a!" but he didn't know what it meant. I said I would Google it to see what it meant. What I found was the Spanish for "Go On" or "Hurry up." Later we were making sock puppets, and Trent said he wanted his sock puppet to have a hat. I said I didn't know how to make a hat for a sock puppet, and he said, "Grandma, get Google on the computer and type in 'sock puppet I need a hat.com.' Arriba, Grandma! Arriba!"

Another time, he and Pat were discussing who was king. Pat said he was king, and Trent said, "no," he was king.

Then he turned to me and said, "Grandma, go to Google and type in 'Who is King—Trent or Grandpa.com?'"

I think my computer slowness was partly responsible for a comment Trent made when he was starting first grade. I asked him if he was eager to go back to school, and he said he was used to vacation and really didn't want to go back. I told him he needed to go to learn so that he could get smarter and smarter. He said, "I want to be as smart as my dad." Pat said, "Well, you'll have to go to school for about 20 years to be that smart."

"How many years will I have to go to be as smart as you, Grandpa?"

"You'll have to go about 30 years to be that smart."

Then Grandpa asked, "How many years do you think you will need to go to school to be as smart as Grandma?"

Trent replied in all seriousness, "Oh, I think I'm already smarter than Grandma."

Remote Control

"Why don't you sit and watch a little television while I clean up the kitchen and get your morning pills?"

I was speaking to my one hundred-year-old mother-in-law, whom I had been caring for the prior few days and who had just finished breakfast. She was sitting in her recliner in the den, unfolding the newspaper for the morning news and her daily cryptogram. It was her favorite place where she could say her morning prayers, watch the television shows she liked and read her magazines. In that recliner, she also talked on the phone, ate many meals, did her physical therapy exercises, balanced her checkbook, created her rainbow and bookmark crafts, wrote greeting cards, and signed checks for her many donations.

"Here are your pills. Let me get the remote here and get the TV on. Maybe Oprah's on or Dr. Phil. Let's see."

Laverne settles back in her recliner, opening the paper, while I push buttons on the remote. "That's funny. I can't seem to get a picture. I'm wondering what's wrong . . . I may have pushed the wrong button when I turned it off last night, but I thought it would be all right today. Hmmm. Do you know how to work it?"

Laverne looks up from the paper. "Did you push the 'cable' button?"

"I think so."

"That's the wrong button. It always gets things mixed up. I can never get it straightened out."

"Oh, boy. I guess I really screwed it up this time . . . Hmm . . . let me call Adele. She should know how to get it going." I get my cell phone, and soon my sister-in-law Adele is on the line.

"Adele, I accidentally turned off the TV with the cable button, and now I can't get back to the regular channels. Your mom wants to watch Oprah, and I can't find her—Oprah I mean. Your mom's right here, but we can't get the regular TV channels."

I repeat Adele's directions: "Okay, try turning the TV off again with the right *off* button, and then turn it on with the right *on* button."

I try it, and it doesn't work.

Adele: "Okay, turn it on with the cable button."

Me: "Sorry, that doesn't work either."

Adele: "Okay, you'll probably have to call the Dish network that handles all the channels. The number should be on the telephone bill—in the file under 'household bills' on the desk in the sunroom behind the computer. By the way, did Mom get a card off to Uncle Cecil for his 94th birthday?"

"Yes, we got the card off yesterday. Okay, I'll try the TV company. Talk to you later."

I finally find the file, rummage through the bills, get the Super Satellite statement with the call number and punch it into my cell phone as I head back to the den. The instructions then begin, "Push 1 for English . . ." About 5 minutes later, Laverne looks up from her paper and asks, "What are you doing?"

"I'm waiting for someone. I think I've finally got the right menu."

"Are we ordering pizza?"

"No, I just want to get the TV turned on so that you can watch Oprah—Oh, yes, hello, I'm calling about our TV. I accidentally turned the television off using the cable button, and now I can't get the regular channels."

"'Turn it off and then back on again?' I'm sorry. I've tried that several times now, and it still doesn't work. Okay, 'turn off the cable box.' Where would that be? . . . Oh, I see it now behind the TV. Can you hold on a minute? I'm going to have to move the couch."

I try to wedge myself between the heavy couch and the TV stand. There is a loud thud.

"Oh, my God, I'm so sorry, Laverne! The couch fell on the floor!"

Laverne seems undisturbed. "Oh, don't worry about it. It's been sitting on cinder blocks for the last year. My friend Shelly stopped last Christmas, and she weighs about 300 pounds, and when she sat down on the couch, the legs broke, so Adele took all the legs off and put the couch on cinder blocks. It falls down from time to time. Don't worry. It will be all right."

I remember the technician. "Hello, I'm sorry. The couch fell on the floor, so I'm going to have to climb over it to get to the cable box. Can you hold on?" There is silence at the other end, and I suddenly realize I am holding the TV remote to my head and speaking into it.

Laverne is pretending not to notice as she looks back at her paper, but is that a slight grin on her face?

I find my phone and repeat the message. The technician is patient and encouraging, "Tell you what. Let's try something else. I want you to find where the TV is plugged in. Then pull out the plug, wait three minutes, and plug it in again."

The plug is behind the couch. Soon I am hanging upside down over the slanting couch, trying to detach the cord from the plug. I get it out, look at my watch for three minutes, plug it back in, and get back on the phone.

"Now," the technician says, "turn on the TV with the right *on* button."

I push the button, and a commercial for Cialis suggests that "the moment is right." I am overjoyed. "It works! It works!" I shout into the phone. "Thank you so much for all of your help!" We say our good-byes, "have a nice day," and then I push *Off* on the phone. That's when I realize that all I did was unplug the TV and plug it back in again, something I could have done on my own. The TV is happily moving from commercial to commercial. Laverne pipes up from her newspaper, "It says here that a penis is coming to town."

"Excuse me?" I suddenly feel as though I've passed into a different universe. I push the "mute" button on the TV, which actually works, thinking I must have misheard what Laverne just said.

"Yes, isn't it great? A penis is coming to town! We haven't had one around here for years!"

"Really?" I say, "A penis?"

"Yes, a penis! He should draw a really big crowd! They have a nice picture of him here, too."

I cross the room and practically snatch the paper from Laverne's hands. A picture of a man in coat and tails appears with the headline: "Pianist to Perform at Pepsi Cola Center."

A month later, I am back at Laverne's and, of course, am scrupulous about my use of the TV remote, but one night after flipping between Rachel Maddow and Sean Hannity to get both the liberal and conservative perspectives on Mitt Romney, I decide to call it a day. I push the power button to turn the TV off. Nothing happens. Rachel is still gesticulating about Mitt's reference to the 47 per cent who don't pay any taxes. I then begin my systematic Plan B—push every button except the cable button, but still Rachel keeps throwing her arms in the air. Okay, what are the options? Turn down the volume, which, fortunately does work, and let the TV continue all night? I worry that the flashing light on the wall in the living room behind the glass doors to the den might disturb Laverne when she wakes in the night. Plan C or is it D—unplug the TV. So once again, though I try to be extra cautious, I am down in the corner stretching to reach behind the couch to unplug the TV when, of course, the couch falls off the cement blocks just as I dislodge the plug from the wall.

I am tired. It has been a long day. I decide to go to bed and deal with it in the morning.

After breakfast when Laverne is sitting in her chair, I explain the couch, now slanting to the south, and I explain the TV. I tell her that although it is a bit inconvenient, the TV should still work when I plug it in, which I proceed to do, being careful not to knock the couch on top of myself. Since there is no sound when I plug in the TV, I figure it is because I have turned the volume down, until I discover, upon rising from the floor, that there is no picture either.

There is nothing. Once again, I push all the buttons but the cable on the remote, and nothing happens. It is nearing time for Laverne's favorite morning soap, and I can't get the TV on.

Maybe it's the batteries in the remote. I change the batteries, say a quick prayer, and try again. This time a picture comes on, but there is no sound. I fiddle with the volume and the mute button. Nothing. I try to turn the TV off and start over, but the power button doesn't work. Laverne is patiently reading the newspaper.

This time I know where the file is that has the number to call for the TV technician, but it is still several minutes before the right buttons bring a live human. This time it is Justin, and he sounds familiar. Did I talk to him the last time? I explain the problem and all the things I've done to fix it.

After a brief pause, Justin says, "It's quite possible the remote has lost its memory."

"The remote has lost its memory," I repeat. Wait, I'm clearly losing my memory, not to mention my mind, but a remote has a memory to lose? I'm thinking of remote Alzheimer's. I'm wondering, could it also be losing its hearing since there is no sound?

"Yes," Justin responds, "I think it's lost its memory. I think we will need to reprogram it."

"Reprogram the remote. Of course, why didn't I think

of that? Sure. Yes, I'm sure we can do that. Uh . . . how do you reprogram a remote?" I'm thinking I might as well be climbing one of those huge rocks where you just reach and hope you grab something. Sisyphus is beginning to take on a whole new meaning in the age of technology.

"Point the remote at the antenna for the cable." So the rigmarole begins. I feel like I'm in an outer space movie. At least ten steps later with various blinking lights, pointing, repetition, and sighs, the TV is now operating with sound.

"Thank you, Justin! You are a life saver!"

"Don't mention it."

The soap is over, Laverne needs to use the commode, it's time for lunch, but the TV is operating.

Three days later I am visiting with Brad, a neighbor, in the den, and I tell him about my experiences with the remote control. While he is commiserating, he reaches over to Laverne's tray table, picks up the remote, and pointing out that his grandchildren have the habit of pushing all the buttons, he demonstrates, before I can grab it out of his hands, how they push all the buttons. The picture on the TV, which was on mute, goes dead. I take the remote from Brad's hand and put it back on Laverne's tray table. Laverne glances up from the rainbow she is making with colored ribbons. Her look says it all, not again! I envision more couch collapses, more calls to the technician, blinking lights, pointing the remote. Then, realizing that I am completely losing even remote control over myself, and wanting to change the subject, I turn to Brad and blurt out, "Did you know that a penis came to town?"

"Yes," Laverne chimes in. "Wasn't that wonderful? I heard he had a big audience!"

Brad is looking at me with a confused frown, and Laverne is suddenly nodding toward the commode, which means that she needs to use it and that I should escort Brad into the kitchen.

"Let's go get some coffee, Brad. We can talk about it in the kitchen." Brad, whose jaw is still hanging, but who has caught Laverne's silent signal, rises and follows me.

I quickly get Brad some coffee, tell him I'll be right back, and go to help Laverne with the commode. As I come into the den, Laverne is already sitting on the commode, watching a live and noisy "Family Feud."

"What happened?"

"Oh, you know, it just comes like that, and you have to go."

"No, I mean with the TV? Brad screwed it up!"

"Oh, I just turned it off and on again a few times. Sometimes that works. Wish I could still do that with my bladder!"

So much for control, remote or not. Technology provides us with the illusion of more and more control, but what we really have power over is still an open question.

In-House Training

My mother had a wonderfully dry sense of humor. She lived to be 104 years old, clear-minded to the end, and over the years, despite the many sorrows she experienced, her humor seemed to sharpen. When she was hospitalized at 103 for surgery and a nurse asked about a bruise on her arm, she didn't hesitate to say in my presence with a wink in my direction, "My daughter hit me." When a nurse's aide later asked her which of the two options she would like for supper, my mom replied, "Oh, dear, just bring me a martini."

The political, social, cultural, technological changes mom lived through from 1905 to 2010 are astounding. In her last years, in particular, the familiar patterns of her thinking and living sometimes contrasted with the technical and advanced know-how of the contemporary age. The disparity at times was quite comical, and mom sometimes delighted in sounding very matter-of-fact in describing the occasional absurdity she experienced, as in this phone conversation we had a few days after she returned to her home from the nursing home after the surgery she had when she was 103.

Mom: Hello. Watch your head there–

Phyllis: Hello, Mom. It's Phyllis. How are you?

Mom: Well, hello, honey! How are you?

Phyllis: I'm fine. Is this a bad time?

Mom: Well, no, it's not bad. It's just that Bob and the baby are crawling around.

Phyllis: Crawling around? Bob and the baby are crawling around? Who's Bob?

Mom: Oh, I'm sorry. Bob McGraw. You know. He lives across the street, and he brought little Ryan over, and you know Ryan–just a minute. Sure, he can have a cookie. Heavens, help yourself! That's what they're there for . . . I'm sorry, honey, how ARE you?

Phyllis: Do you want me to call you back?

Mom: No, no, that's all right. I have time now while they're crawling. You know that's the latest technique from Pathways, I think it is. Ryan doesn't know how to crawl very well yet, you know. He's only 8 months old. Anyway, you're supposed to get down on the floor and show him how, so Bob brings him over here where there isn't much to get into, and then he gets down on the floor and shows Ryan how. So now they're in the bathroom. I guess there's the tiger crawl and the crab crawl and the bunny hop, I think. I forget all the kinds. It can take quite a while, and I don't like to watch television while they're doing it, so it's fine. I'm glad you called!

Phyllis: You have a man and a baby crawling around your house, and now they're in the bathroom?

Mom: Shhh. It's not how it sounds. I mean, he's just helping the baby, and they're just crawling around. You know we never helped any of you kids when you were learning to crawl. I guess you just taught yourselves. Wait, here they come. Hold on, honey . . . you can move that chair if it's in the way, Bob. Just be careful of the lamp. I'd hate for him to get hurt. What did you say, honey?

Phyllis: I didn't say anything. I'm waiting for the crawling man to move through the living room.

Mom: Oh, they're crawling into the kitchen now—Bob, I'm not sure how clean that floor is. Be careful out there! . . . What did you say, honey?

Phyllis: Maybe I should call back later.

Mom: No, that's all right. They're gone for now. It will take them awhile to get through the kitchen and the bathroom again and then through the bedroom and then back into the living room. Oh, I was going to tell you that the . . . oh, what's she called? Some kind of therapist came today from the hospital I think or the nursing home.

Phyllis: A physical therapist?

Mom: No, I don't remember what she's called. It sounded more like an architectural therapist.

Phyllis: Architectural therapist? Oh, do you mean an occupational therapist?

Mom: Yes, that's it! That's what she called herself, but I don't know why since I don't have any occupation. Anyway, she came while Barbara and Kermit were here. Someone sent her to be sure I could live here on my own. I guess they have to do that for anyone released from the nursing home to be sure they can live on their own. I told her that Barbara and Kermit come to help every week, and Keeran stops by every day. And that I've been living on my own for over thirty years, but since I had that surgery for the blocked intestine and since I'm 103, I guess they thought I needed someone to see if I could do things on my own. Even though I spent those six weeks in the nursing home, and I did all right there! I don't think I even needed to go there.

Phyllis: Well, Mom, they just wanted to be sure you could live on your own after the surgery. So, what did the occupational therapist do when she was there?

Mom: Well, first she wanted me to show her how I can make toast. She was very young, and I think I was her first patient or client or whatever I am, so I wanted to help her as much as I could, but I told her I never eat toast; I get those crumbs under my plate, you know, and it's just such a nuisance! I just keep the toaster out for overnight guests. And they can make their own. But I guess I had to prove to her that I could make toast if I wanted it, so I put the bread in the toaster, and we made toast. I wanted her to eat it because I don't eat toast, and I hate to waste food, but she said she wasn't hungry, so Barbara said she would take it home to feed the birds, but the girl wanted to be sure I could butter it if I ever made it, so I had to butter it first, and you know with my arthritis, that isn't the easiest thing to do, but I managed pretty well if I do say so myself . . . Oh, just a minute. Bob, be careful in there. I was going through old pictures in the bedroom, and they're in a box on the floor. Oh, they're all over the floor now? Well, Keeran will pick them up when he comes. Where was I?

Phyllis: You just made the toast. Did the O.T. have you do anything else?

Mom: The O.T.? Oh, you mean the young girl. Yes, all kinds of things. I had to write a check, even though Keeran or Barbara always do that for me, and she tore it up when I was done, and those things cost money! And what else? Oh, I had to make coffee, even though I had already had my two cups and didn't want any more. And she didn't want any coffee, and Barbara and Kermit didn't want any, so now I have a pot of coffee I don't need, so I'll have to warm that coffee up tomorrow . . . No, Bob, it's all right. Don't worry about it. Barbara will put all the underwear back in the drawer. I didn't realize we left that bottom drawer open . . . What did you say, honey?

Phyllis: Really, Mom, I should call you back.

Mom: Well, that's fine, but I have to tell you about

the most interesting thing the uh, the young girl made me do. She had me look up Fleet Farm or Menard's, I can't remember which it was, in the phone book. Then I had to call them, ask for the paint department, and order a gallon of paint. I told her I hadn't planned on doing any house painting soon, but I guess it is part of their job to make sure I can look up phone numbers and order over the phone if I ever need to, but I never do because Barbara and Kermit and Keeran take care of everything I need. I felt so sorry for that paint salesman because he had to go through a list of possibilities and make recommendations, and then I decided on something—I think it was Polar Bear white with eggshell primer, doesn't that sound nice? But lo and behold, after I picked out the paint, the young girl took the phone and told the salesman this was just a test for me to see if I could order paint on my own, even though I would never need to do that. I think that's why I thought she was an architectural therapist. I wanted to call that man after she left and tell him I would take the paint I was ordering.

Phyllis: Mom, are you serious? Did this really happen?

Mom: Yes, that poor salesman, but it did make me think maybe I should have the kitchen repainted. What do you think? Anyway the young girl said it was probably all right if I lived on my own if I had a lot of help. Of course, I told her that I have a lot of help to begin with, but . . .

Oh, Bob, what's that? No, I'm sorry, I do have diapers, but I don't have any baby ones . . . Sure you can come back with Ryan anytime . . . Just close the door behind you . . . Where were we, honey?

Language Designs

Weaving Words

As a veteran crocheter, I have often had to deal with broken thread or yarn, unravel rows of miscounted stitches, or try to untangle thread that has become knotted. Sometimes, I've seen unintended patterns emerge from freelance pieces I have been working on. In a somewhat similar way, I have become amazed at how intricate language can be–how it can be used to provide elaborate escapes from reality, how it can generate labyrinthine paths that sometimes seem to lead nowhere, how it can stir up numerous threads in multiple directions, and how it sometimes creates patterns of its own without the speaker or writer even realizing it.

I have always been fascinated by language. I majored in French and English as an undergraduate, obtained a masters degree in Comparative Literature, and finally focused on English language and literature for my doctorate. Between 1963 and 2006, I taught on and off for over thirty years at five different high schools and three different colleges. I thoroughly enjoyed studying and teaching, and as the years went by, I jotted down notes from various episodes that I found interesting and humorous. Although I had some brilliant students, stimulating classes, wonderful colleagues, hard-working peers and students, it was the occasional class diversions, unproductive meetings, and my own idiosyncrasies that I found myself jotting down, sharing with colleagues, and later adding to this collection. The fascinating patterns that emerge when we try to communicate with one another provide an endless source for contemplation, amazement, and sometimes great delight.

Literary Criticism

When I was a graduate student working on my doctoral dissertation on Samuel Beckett's writings and doing research at the University of Texas in Austin in the late 1970s, a Beckett conference was being held there, and although I had no paper to present, I was invited, as a student, to sit in on the sessions. I'll never forget the opening one.

The convener was a renowned Beckett scholar who welcomed all the Beckett academics. They had come not only from numerous states but also from Canada, England, Ireland, and France. In the course of his welcoming remarks, he included a short greeting from Samuel Beckett himself, who was advised of the conference and invited to attend. The note read briefly to the effect, "Thank you for your invitation. I cannot attend. I wish you well. All the best, Samuel Beckett."

Immediately after the convener read the note, a hand went up from another noted Beckett scholar. The man stood up, turned his back to the speaker and announced to the group: "Obviously, Beckett is being satiric here. He hates critics. He would never wish us well."

An uncomfortable pause followed, while the host reassembled his remarks, but then another hand shot up. "I don't think Beckett was being satiric. I think that psychoanalytically, his note makes a lot of sense: subconsciously, he wants us to fail, but consciously, he doesn't want to impede our work, which brings his writing more recognition."

"Wait." A woman in the back row rose: "The note itself is a typical male response: 'I'm the one this conference is all about. I can't be bothered coming to see you. Carry on your drudgery; just don't bother me.'"

I was tempted to stand up and say that I thought what Beckett wrote was actually what he wanted to say, but I was a comparative novice in Beckett studies, and it seemed completely naive at the time.

Then another attendee with eye glasses and a goatee piped up, "Wait a minute. Let's not get carried away." For a moment I hoped he was going to express my thoughts, but he went on, "We're not even sure Beckett wrote this note. He could have told someone else to respond for him and merely signed it, if, in fact, he did sign it. And if he did—that is, actually write the note and actually signed it—was he even thinking, or was he just performing a routine duty? How many requests does he get in a day?"

"I have to agree with that to a degree. I've actually met Beckett," an elderly man offered, pausing for the audience to take in his own privileged status, "I was in Paris and by accident, I ran into him on Rue Bonaparte. I introduced myself, and he wished me luck in my work after a very quick conversation. I think he was trying to get rid of me, but he was pleasant for a moment, which is what he seems to be trying to do in this note."

"But notice his language," an elderly woman followed up. "He said 'I *cannot* attend.' Not 'I *will not* attend.' Is he ill or incapable of travel? Or is he an artist who wants no part in the interpretation of his work? The words he uses are important!"

"I'm sorry," said an elderly gentleman with a French accent, "but this entire conversation is *inutile,* beside the point. We all know that Beckett is the author *sans pareil* of the theatre of the absurd. The note isn't satiric or ironic or dismissive. His note is, how do you say, a *paradigm* of his drama: meaningless."

By the time the discussion was finished, the welcome was ended, and the conference was formally begun, I was totally confused, and the conference itself did not do much to clear things up.

A few years later, while I was finishing my work on my dissertation, I came across a French poem that Beckett had written early in his writing career that I wanted to use as an introduction to my analysis. Although I could translate it myself, I thought Beckett's own translation would be more revealing, so I took the chance and wrote to him in Paris to see if he would consider translating the poem into English. To my surprise, he responded immediately with a hand-written note: "Dear Ms. Carey, Thank you for your letter. I could not translate that poor poem. Not even the heart to try. Please forgive. Best Wishes, Samuel Beckett."

Later, when I was completing my dissertation, I came across comments by literary critics suggesting that James Joyce had referred indirectly to Beckett in *Finnegans Wake*, but the date of the quote and Joyce's acquaintance with Beckett seemed to contradict each other, so I wrote again to Beckett in Paris, asking him about the discrepancy. He wrote back immediately: "Thank you for yrs. of Jan 20. I first met Joyce late 28. The passage cannot refer to me.

With all good wishes, Yours sincerely, Samuel Beckett."

I treasure those notes and have no doubt that a few years before, Beckett was simply sending his regrets and wishing the Beckett conference-goers well. Sometimes when we dissect language for hidden agendas and ulterior motives, we destroy the simple but nevertheless genuine and lovely patterns of meaning that are right there on the surface.

Student Papers

From my many years of teaching English on the high school and college levels, I corrected thousands of papers and managed to save some unique tidbits from student writings. While the students were expressing ideas that were clear to them, the words they chose sometimes evoked startling images. Here are a few samples with my immediate, then unexpressed responses:

"You can't imagine how excited I was when I saw the Eyefull Tower in London." [*You're right! It's beyond my imagination in many ways!*]

"We enjoyed the relaxation of water sports, leisurely walks, and nightly bombfires." [*Hope you slept well!*]

"If I quit smoking, I may change the Surgeon General's

estimate of 390,000 lives claimed from smoking to 391,000 American lives." [*You might also want to consider taking MATH 101.*]

"I hope to go to college to pursue a courier." [*Why don't you just go out for track?*]

"Women should not be put down by their male piers." [*Especially if they're not wearing life jackets.*]

"For the prom, I wore a shining sequence dress with the back out. Mark had on a tuxedo with a matching concubine." [*Now that's what I call a fashion statement!*]

"I just hope that with working and taking classes, I don't put my kids on the back burner." [*I hope so, too!*]

"I think my sister is suffering from post-mortem depression." [*Oh, dear, I don't think there's a treatment for that.*]

Orientation to College

Incoming first-year college students come from a variety of economic, ethnic, religious, and educational backgrounds. First-year orientation is an attempt to draw these differing threads together to form a communal understanding of the mission of the college, the standards of conduct, benefits available, grading system, etc. Because of the diversity of student backgrounds, however, the initial attempt to form a cohesive understanding of the college's offerings is sometimes challenging. Language sometimes takes precedence over ideas, one word evoking another association, and the movement goes from one experience to another. "Herding cats" is an idiom often associated with trying to bring together a disparate group into a cohesive whole, but I have coined my own expression: "Unravelling a basket of tangled yarn." It takes work, but you learn to appreciate the individual strands in the process.

Prof. C: "Today we want to talk about health care and counseling services here at the college. The assignment you read for today's class deals directly with that issue—'Health Issues for the College Student.' Yes, Judy?"

Judy: "I have a friend who has a health care issue. She had this huge boil on her nose, and when she picked it, it got all scabby and everything, and like, she wanted to go to the doctor, but her health insurance doesn't cover boils."

Helen: "I had a boil once, and it got so bad, I had to go see a doctor, but he said there wasn't anything that could be done about it. It just had to heal by itself."

Cher: "Don't you just hate it when the people who are supposed to be treating you don't do it? Are you supposed to treat yourself? What if that boil had gotten infected?"

Keena: "I think you have to look at both sides of it

though. What if the doctor treated the boil and it didn't heal right, and he could have faced a malpractice suit. I mean, what about the doctor's side? I'm not saying he was right. I'm just saying you have to think about it."

Liz: "I suppose this is an awful thing to say, but I personally hate boils. I mean, I have always . . . really . . . hated . . . boils."

Prof. C: "Well, we were talking about health care and college, and there really are some serious issues here. That's why it's one of the topics in our Orientation Class. One aspect we need to discuss is health issues and college expenses. Yes, Helen?"

Helen: "My cousin Fred moved here from Ohio, and he couldn't find a job. He went to apply at one place, and they told him they were going to hire him, but when he went back, they pretended like they didn't even know who he was. It was so weird."

Judy: "That happened to me once. I was a sophomore in high school, and I was promised a job at McDonald's, and the very day I was supposed to start work, they called me and said like 'We don't need you after all.' I mean it was sooo rude."

Cher: "But really, think about it. Most of those fast food chains don't even have health insurance for their employees."

Liz: "Well, who would want it at McDonald's? I mean, that food is so bad. I never eat there if I can avoid it."

Helen: "Yeah, but Taco Bell's even worse. Did I tell you I stopped there after work one night and ordered the chicken fajitas, and all three of us in the car—every one of us—threw up."

Prof. C: "Uh, I'm wondering if we could just focus on the main issue here—health care and college. Some colleges do not offer health care to students, and that's an important issue. Some Americans do not believe that all people have a right to health care. We'll talk about that later, but . . . yes, Cher?"

Cher: "I think that's really important to think about. You know, what if everyone didn't think anyone had a right to anything? I mean, think about it."

Keena: Well, that was the point I was trying to make before. I mean, some people think everyone has a right to everything, and some people don't think anyone has any rights, so you have to look at it both ways.

Helen: Well, I don't know if this is what you mean, but in South Dakota, someone in government just said that everyone should carry a gun. Can you believe that? I can't even afford an IPhone4!

Judy: Oh, I know this may be off the topic just a little, but I just got one of those. You won't believe all the apps it's got. I mean, it has Facebook and Twitter and Instagram and Uber—I could show you after class if you want to check it out. OMG, it is so hot!

Cher: But seriously, most of us can't afford an IPhone4. I can hardly manage to pay for the books I need for class—

Prof. C: Excuse me, if I could remind you—the topic we want to discuss today is the issue of health care and college. Are you aware of the services that this college offers both for physical and mental health? Uh, yes, Liz?

Liz: I know this isn't exactly on the topic, but well, my family moved three years ago from Wauwatosa to Brookfield, and I don't know about health care, but the shopping in Brookfield is a whole lot better . . .

Writing across the Curriculum

Committee and curriculum meetings on the college level sometimes provide fascinating designs as highly-educated people try to communicate across their disciplines. Trying to mesh expertise from different disciplines for the good of students illustrates the interlocking patterns that sometimes emerge.

"We are here," I began, as I looked at the six professors seated around the table, "to get a sense of the written and oral communication skills of the students you teach in the Art Department and to see how we can better improve those skills. You each have a set of the questions we want to discuss. So shall we begin? Let's start with some basic information. What kinds of written and oral work do you give your students in their art classes?"

The professors shift in their chairs. Carl takes out a handkerchief and begins mopping his brow. Connie shuffles her papers. Clarice peers suspiciously from under her thick eyebrows. I smile and look from face to face, desperately willing someone to open his or her mouth and practice some oral skills.

"Well, in art," Therese begins, "we, of course, put great emphasis on the visual as a way of communication." Some heads begin to nod in agreement. "Line and perspective are extremely important. And, of course, color and hue." Carl looks straight at me and begins nodding his head from side to side in clear disagreement. "Students, of course, have to speak about their work," Therese continues. "And sometimes I have them write about their work, but they don't always use correct grammar and punctuation."

"Why is it," Martin interjects, "these students can't write? Don't they teach them in grade school and high school anymore? I remember having to diagram sentences. We knew what every word was in those sentences. We learned nouns and verbs and all those other grammar terms . . ."

"They learn these things; they just don't use them," Clarice chimes in.

"Well, I'm not so sure they are taught all the basic writing skills—" Janice, my colleague in the interview, offers.

"Don't tell me what they learn," Clarice snaps. "I taught high school English before teaching art on the college level, and I know what they learned."

Janice turns scarlet and begins tapping her foot. She looks like she is going to either run out of the room or start crying.

"Well, everyone knows," Martin says in mounting excitement, "good readers are good writers. But the students don't read any more. What if we gave them a book to read? Say, *Moby Dick.* Do they read *Moby Dick* anymore? Do they even know who Moby Dick was? And some artists also wrote. We could give them a book written by an artist, and then maybe they would write better!"

"Harriet Carlson is a good writer," Carl joins in. "She was in my 'Color and Design' course. Margaret Roper writes well, too. Did you have her in class?" Carl is looking directly at me, but it is clearly a rhetorical question. "Of course, not all of us use concepts like 'color' and 'hue,'" Carl goes on, glancing sideways at Therese. "You have to take the students where they are, and some of them aren't ready for concepts–you have to take them where they are. You have to start with lines . . ."

"I personally don't have time to teach writing," Linda says, as though she were the only person in the room and talking to a movie projector. "They're supposed to learn writing in their English classes. I can't correct their writing. I'm not a professional writing critic. I don't even have time to correct papers. Maybe we should give our papers to the English Department to correct." A noticeable current seems to be stirring.

"I think Goya wrote some, and didn't Rembrandt keep a diary?" Martin is gaining energy.

"It seems to me that some students are perfectly capable of dealing with color and hue."

"Martin, you're thinking of Monet."

"Why don't they teach them how to diagram sentences?"

"When I taught high school, students learned how to write."

"Well, even if they read *Moby Dick*, it would be an improvement. Do they even know who Moby Dick was?"

Student Advising

"So, what's new, Melissa?"

"Well, you know, Dr. Carey, the most incredible thing has happened, and I just want to explore my options to see how long it will take me to graduate. You see, Larry and I,—Larry's the guy I've been seeing for the last few years—well, over the break we got together, and you'll never believe this. I still can't believe it, but anyway, he is being transferred to Omaha! At least, they are sending him there temporarily for the time being—I mean his company is sending him. It's ML&B, a huge public relations business, and I don't know if I told you or not but my ex—you know Marty, well, we were only married for three years. Anyway, Marty finally got a job—he was hired as a consultant or something, so he can start sending me money again. I can't believe how broke I am, and the girls, too, of course, but anyway, Larry's ex surprised him at Christmas by announcing out of the blue that she just got remarried. Can you believe it? They've only been officially divorced for six months! But anyway, so now he doesn't have to pay her alimony anymore, which makes his money situation look a lot better, but his sons are really upset that their mom got married again. Do you know they never even met her new husband? I can't believe how tacky that is! It's just so strange to get remarried without even letting your kids know who their new step-dad is! Larry has spent a lot of time with me and the girls, so they know him pretty well. I guess Marty and his new wife, I think her name is Carla, anyway they eloped or something. Well, anyway, when I was out in California with Larry, even though he didn't propose, I'm thinking he may want me to go to Omaha with him, and so I thought I should come and talk to you. What I'm wondering about is if I and the girls were to go to Omaha with him, could I take a course there and have it transferred here, or do you think independent study would be better?"

By the time Melissa finishes, I realize the complex patterns in life that many contemporary students are living. The question of independent study or course transfer suddenly becomes a tiny loop in a much more serious maze of interconnections. When I see the twists and tangles in the lives of young people today, the designs my life has taken seem so much more uncomplicated. The notion of "student advising" takes on a whole new meaning. Where do you begin?

Unintended Side Effects

One day a student came to my writing class with a swollen face and glazed eyes. I asked her what the problem was, and she told me she was suffering from the side effects of an anti-allergy medication she was taking.

"Wait a minute," I said. "What kind of effects do you have from the allergy itself?"

"Well," she said, "I think it's the pollen. It makes my eyes really itchy and red, and then I usually puff up all over, and I can't concentrate without the meds."

The effects of the medication were not unlike the symptoms she was experiencing before she took it. I was reminded of the warning that came with the bottle of Citalbien I had recently been prescribed for temporary, mild depression, "Side effects may include a decrease in sexual desire or ability; diarrhea; dizziness; drowsiness; dry mouth; increased sweating; lightheadedness when you stand or sit up; loss of appetite; nausea; stuffy nose; tiredness" and, a paragraph later, "suicidal thoughts or attempts; tremor; unusual bruising or bleeding; unusual or severe mental or mood changes; unusual weakness; vision changes; worsening of depression." Needless to say, I opted for a hot bath and a glass of wine.

But back to unintended side effects. As an English teacher, I have become increasingly aware of how punctuation, spelling, grammar and usage when used incorrectly can have unintended consequences and misleading results, like the missing comma in the sentence, "Let's eat Grandma!" I love to see the patterns language takes by itself when the speaker/writer may not be aware. Let me illustrate further. Take the distinction between "which" and "that." Now, although there are at least two schools of thought on the difference between "which" and "that," (one grammar book suggests it is a false distinction while another points out that any truly educated person should know the difference and use the terms correctly), one intended side effect of discussing the distinction in class is to raise consciousness (or is it "consciousnesses" or even "consciences"?) of the sometimes subtle ways that imprecise language can be used in misleading, and/or deceitful, and/or even manipulative ways.

For example, in the 1980s, William Safire wrote a great column called "The Wicked Which and the Comma" (*New York Times*, Sept. 2, 1984) that showed how a "which" was used without a comma and, therefore, suggested that Republicans in a particular election were not opposed to raising taxes but rather to raising only certain kinds of taxes. Now, the average voter probably knows that where American politicians stand on particular issues is about as relevant as what Jack the Ripper preferred for breakfast. No, wait, Jack liked "Shredded" Wheat. Sorry, couldn't resist. Isn't language fun? But getting back to Safire's example, if the politicians knew what they were saying, and they were saying it intentionally, they might have been trying to mislead someone—no way! Politics notwithstanding, however, the "which/that" distinction can be crucial to daily intercourse (or bi-weekly, or whatever your preference).

Say, for example, I told you, "I like eating fruit, which is good for your health" (well, maybe good for *my* health, or good for *one's* health). What would the difference be if I said, "I like eating fruit *that* is good for your health"? Do you hear the difference? In the first sentence, I am suggesting that I like to eat fruit in general, and fruit in general is considered good for your/my/our health. In the second sentence, I'm saying that I like to eat only fruit that is good for my own health. The latter sentence suggests that some fruit may not be good for my health, and I will eat only that kind of fruit that *is* good (for my health, of course, not just good fruit). Note, I do not say "only eat" because that would suggest that I would not drink, inhale, or otherwise imbibe fruit that is good for my health. "Only" is one of my favorite adverbs and can lead to all kinds of side effects, usually quite amusing. For example, if you said, "I only have sex with my husband"–if that's *all* you do with your husband, despite the monogamy, I don't have a lot of hope for this marriage! Now if you said, "I have sex only with my husband," that's another thing entirely. Isn't language fun?

But back to "that" and "which." The point here is that "that" is restrictive, and "which" is non-restrictive. Now, what does that mean? Well, here is where the comma plays a huge role. Let's hear it for commas! They are probably the most underestimated punctuation mark in any language, and yet the mighty comma (or lack thereof) can make a huge difference! "Which" clauses are always preceded and followed by commas, which means that the information added is explanatory or supplemental but non-essential, as in this very sentence. "That" clauses are not preceded by a comma because the "that" clause designates or restricts exactly what we're talking about. Let's look at an example: The cows that are in the pasture are headed to market (not the cows that are in the barn). The "that" restricts/defines exactly which cows we are talking about. Many times the "that" is just understood, e.g., "the cows in the pasture." The cows, which are in the pasture, are headed to market (all the cows are going to market, and, by the way, they are in the pasture—the "which" adds only nonessential information). Wasn't that easy?

But what difference does any of this make? Well, for one thing, if you know the distinction, you will produce fewer unintended side effects. By the way, do you know the difference between "fewer" and "less"? Don't you just hate it when the sign at the grocery store says "15 Items or Less"? By the way, do you know how to use semi-colons effectively? But back to "which" and "that." What's important in this whole discussion is that if you can distinguish between restrictive and non-restrictive elements, you can produce more intentional and desirable effects in your own use of language.

That little comma that separates non-restrictive from restrictive elements makes a lot of difference, not just in "which" and "that" clauses but in many other cases as well. I like to think I make the most out of that comma, especially when it isn't there. For example, I like to tell my nieces and nephews that I'm their favorite Aunt Phyllis. If I added the comma, I would be saying that I'm their favorite aunt of all their aunts, and Phyllis is my name. Without the comma, I am their favorite Aunt Phyllis of all their aunts named Phyllis, and since I am their *only* Aunt Phyllis, I know it is absolutely true. "Dear favorite nephew Randy." "Hi, favorite niece Amy" and "favorite niece Angie," etc. (I have twenty-seven nieces and nephews, and they're all my favorites individually; by the way, do you know the differences between "there, their and they're"?) Since I don't have duplicate nieces and nephews with these names (or nieces and nephews with duplicate names), I am being both honest and loving. At this point, the whole family knows my preferences (eccentricities, obsessions, etc.), and I usually use just acronyms: FNA (favorite nephew Aaron), FNJ, FNS, FNL, etc.

Okay, it's true that when I first started using the "favorite aunt" tag, people got a little upset. Nieces and nephews became a little uncomfortable because some of them may have actually liked one of my sisters better than me (impossible for me to believe, but note, grammatically, "better than they liked me"), and they (my nieces and nephews) may have thought I was usurping their choices, but once they understood the difference the lack of a comma made, I became "favorite Aunt Phyllis" since I am their only Aunt Phyllis. In fact, because many of them also seem to be into acronyms, I am "FAP" to most of my nieces and nephews, which is both flattering and a bit uncomfortable for me but much better than "FLAP" (favorite, lovable Aunt Phyllis), but as you now know by the "which" clause, my feelings on the subject are non-essential, additional information, although I do feel a slightly greater twinge when my sister-in-law uses the acronym she has come up with for me—Favorite Oldest Sister-in-Law (FOSIL). My brother Keith never got into the "favorite uncle" thing; I suspect he just didn't want to deal with the acronym in his case.

The secret, of course, is to restrict descriptions so that they can refer to only one person; for example, YFYS means "your favorite youngest sister" to my older sisters and my older brother. One of my sisters extended her acronym a bit: OOYFOS- "one of your favorite older sisters" and I could use that one for my initials when addressing my younger brother, but I prefer the shorter YFSP (your favorite sister Phyllis). I admit that I have an unusual affinity for acronyms and can sometimes sense their presence in places you might not suspect. For example, do you realize that the acronym for Unintended Side Effects is USE! While you're reading the list of terrible potential results of taking a particular drug, the acronym is shouting out, "USE!" What kind of subliminal advertising is that?

By now, you may be thinking, "this woman is really loco" (TWIRL) or even less complimentary thoughts, but in my own humble opinion, I think I'm simply using the nuances in language effectively. Just ask my favorite son Brian or my favorite son Michael. Of course, if I put a comma in either of those expressions—"my favorite son, Brian" or "my favorite son, Michael"—I would never hear the end of it! Likewise, if I had only one favorite cousin out of my thirty-eight cousins, my favorite cousin, Connie, for instance, I would be in a heap of trouble.

And, of course, the whole country is into acronyms. Did you watch the SOTU by the POTUS? ICE isn't just something you put in your drinks anymore! Just ask DACA! And look at the acronyms on Facebook and Twitter-LOL, LMHO, OMG, ROTFLOL, FYEO, TMI. Okay, I may be a professor with a slight case of OCD, but let's get back to commas.

Finally, in rare instances, the lack of a comma can have an intended effect of flattering the person referred to and at the same time an unintended side effect (and here, I'm not being redundant) of raising a few questions, acronyms notwithstanding. When my husband, Pat, (note the commas because I have only one husband, and his name is additional information), who is also a professor, published his first book, he dedicated it "To my wife Phyllis." I can't tell you how proud and thrilled I was! Who wouldn't be elated to receive a book dedication! But if you've followed the previous discussion and understand the difference the comma makes, you can already see the problem. If one has a sensitive understanding of commas (SUC), questions arise in one's mind: Did Pat pick Phyllis because she is his favorite wife? Which of his wives will he dedicate his next book to? (Of course, you should ordinarily never end a sentence with a preposition as I just did.)

All this by way of saying, punctuation, usage, and grammar are important, and unintended side effects can be avoided in language, at least some of the time–IYKWIM. Isn't language fun?

Grace

Everything is Something

"Isn't that something!" I said in amazement about the glowing field of dandelions we were passing in the car.

"Everything is something, Grandma." Six-year-old Trent responded from his car seat to my spontaneous awe. He was right, of course, but I was more aware of the echo I heard in the words "everything is something." In my memory, it was suddenly summer, 1974, in Ireland. Pat and I had taken a sightseeing bus to Glendalough with Tom, a man in his forties from London and his seven-year-old daughter, Grainne, who were staying at the same Bed and Breakfast in Dublin. In Glendalough, we were looking at the tiny church where Kevin stood, where, the guide informed us, St. Kevin put his arms out the windows and a blackbird landed on his open hand and laid an egg while he prayed. He kept his arms extended through the windows of his small cell until the eggs hatched and the baby birds took flight. It was twenty-two years before Seamus Heaney's "St. Kevin and the Blackbird," a poem that would encapsulate like the egg shell the mystery of life giving life in still wonder.

"Isn't that something!" I had said then, as I usually did when I was amazed.

"Of course, everything is some *thing*!" Grainne responded in her proper English accent, belying her Irish name, red curly hair and freckled face, and conveying her total disdain of an adult who could be so stupid.

I wondered about Grainne now—she would be mid-forties if she were still living. Her father had told Pat and me in hushed tones that he had brought Grainne to Ireland after a messy divorce. Her mother was overly protective and limited his visits. Looking back now, I thought about child abduction. Why hadn't we notified the authorities? Why had we just moved on to another Irish town and another Bed and Breakfast? Maybe Grainne's mother was protecting Grainne for a reason? The little girl seemed content and happy; but maybe Tom was abusive, or maybe he wasn't really her father.

"It's none of our business."

"He seems like a nice enough fellow."

"He is very open about the situation."

"We don't know what the truth is."

At the time, it seemed best to stay out of it—we were in our twenties on a delayed honeymoon, hitchhiking in Ireland in the seventies in a world that no longer exists, but Grainne still traveled in my memory. When in the 90s, I read Seamus Heaney's poem, "St. Kevin and the Blackbird," my first response was "isn't that something!" I was amazed by the music of the poetry, the memory of the story, the mental image of Glendalough, an outstretched hand nurturing new life, and a precocious seven-year-old child, wandering in a foreign country with a man who claimed to be her father. For a moment, I found myself "linked/ into the network of eternal life" through wonder of the fragile threads that interweave our memories and our lives. Everything *is* something, even if we can't see all that it is.

Fast forward to the present, and we were merging onto I-43 north on our hour commute to Green Bay.

"Do you feel like a snooze, honey?"

"No, Grandma. I just got up from my nap about ten minutes ago. Let's play a game."

"A Great Job"

My sister RoseAnn realized she was sick on Valentine's Day, 2001. I didn't realize it until a week later when she e-mailed me that she had planned to go on a retreat but had to cancel because of the flu. Then we found out over that weekend that she was in the hospital with a fever. The next weekend, I worried as she went through test after test. She thought she was in the clear, but then the doctors decided to do a liver biopsy because of scar tissue on her liver, and we found out on March 2 that she had liver cancer. At that time, according to her husband, Ivan, the doctors said she had six months to a year to live and recommended chemotherapy.

I took our then ninety-six-year-old mother on the four-hour drive to see RoseAnn the weekend of March 10. I will never forget how RoseAnn looked when she saw that mom had made the trip. I know that my bringing Mom to her that weekend was the best gift I had ever given her. RoseAnn was still nauseous and resting a lot, but I was able to give her a back rub. Ivan and I put on a terrible violin recital, but RoseAnn didn't mind how awful we sounded. Her daughter, Angie, was there, so we were able to visit with her and help take care of her mom. The trip seemed like a pure gift from my dad, who had died thirty years before, also from cancer. I knew from the day that I heard RoseAnn's diagnosis that it would go very fast. I don't know how I knew, maybe from what Dad had experienced.

RoseAnn had the first bout of chemo but went through such nausea that she was quite miserable and dehydrated. They never really got the nausea under total control. She threw up a large amount the day before she died.

She decided on the Monday of Holy Week (April 9th) that she would not do any more chemo. She was already so sick that she couldn't face any more. I had gone home to make arrangements to return, and then I returned that Wednesday. Our oldest sister, JoAn, had come in the night before. Barbara, another sister, and our mother came later that day. From Wednesday to Friday we visited with her on and off. Her spirits were good. We had some good laughs and some happy reminiscing. When I was rubbing her back, she told me to send an e-mail to JoAn and Barbara after she was gone, saying that now she had Dad all to herself. And if all worked out, she would have Mom and Dad a long time to herself before any of the rest of us joined them. My favorite line came when I mentioned (for the tenth time) that I used to work as a nurse's aide. RoseAnn said to JoAn, "JoAn, did you ever work . . .?"

We had a wonderful prayer service with Father Mike, who did an anointing, and Mom led a decade of the rosary when Pat, Ivan, and I were there. My husband, Pat, had driven from Manitowoc to Omaha on Holy Thursday. During the anointing, the loudspeakers played "Lullaby and Good Night," the song that indicates a new baby was born:

Lullaby, and good night, in the skies stars are bright
May the moon, silvery beams, bring you with dreams
Close your eyes, now and rest, may these hours be blessed
Till the sky's bright with dawn, when you wake with a yawn.

We heard the melody often while RoseAnn was there, and Mom asked her to sing it. She sang it for my mom. I wonder if it was the last time she sang. Her voice was beautiful and strong, and it seemed like a lullaby of new birth both into this life and into heaven.

The whole immediate family came to see her during that week. Pat and I and Mom said goodbye on Good Friday, and we took Mom back to Iowa. Mom told her how well she was doing. It meant so much to RoseAnn. I think she understood all that it implied. I was afraid we would not see her again in this life. Pat and I went back to Wisconsin on Holy Saturday, but when I talked to Ivan on Monday, I told him I had to come back. I flew back in on Wednesday morning. RoseAnn was home on hospice, but she was in some pain. The RN on duty talked to Ivan and me about the stages in dying and indicated that it wouldn't be long. When I talked to JoAn later that day, I told her that she should come right away. In one of my bad spells, Eric, RoseAnn's younger son, came into the kitchen, and we just held each other and wept. Ivan, too, had several weeping spells. On Thursday morning, April 19th, I felt that it would be the day RoseAnn would leave us. I called Mom and held the phone to RoseAnn's ear so that Mom could speak to her although RoseAnn at that time was unable to speak. Then I called Barbara and did the same. I wiped RoseAnn's face often and her hands. I told her I loved her, how much her and Ivan's adopting of Angie and Eric had meant to Pat and me. It had given us the courage to adopt our two sons. I told her that she was much loved. Our sister JoAn got there around noon. Then three of RoseAnn's friends came, and the priest came again for the anointing. Her son Aaron was also there. We all stood around her as she was anointed, and then Mary, Bev, and Virginia led a decade of the rosary. Then JoAn sang her a Celtic lullaby, and we all sang "An Irish Lullaby," "Amazing Grace," and "When Irish Eyes are Smiling" although we couldn't remember all the words. Shortly after that, the morphine pump had an occlusion. I went to hold it while the nurse assistant called the RN. I was standing near RoseAnn's head holding her hand and the morphine pump, and JoAn was there as well, when there was a change in her breathing. I called for Ivan, and one of the women went to get him, but then RoseAnn opened her eyes and looked straight at me. It was an indescribable look—her eyes were so clear. And they reminded me of Dad's eyes—she looked so much like Grandma Knight. Even though one of her eyes was a prosthesis, I never thought of that at the time. They seemed like true eyes that were seeing so clearly. Then she closed her eyes. I know I said, "go with God," and "we love you, RoseAnn," but I don't remember much else. Aaron said, "You did a great job, Mom." I think it referred to her whole life, but it couldn't have described her leaving any better.

Dad

When I visit your grave,
I always look for a sign
That you live yet somewhere,
That your spirit goes on
Beyond my famished hopes.

A stubborn dandelion in August—
A June flock of geese—
It doesn't take much.
I feed my hunger
On nature's morsels.

Today with no sign
I turn away,
Only to meet in the morning sun—
The glistening, frosty shadow
Of your tombstone
Etched in green grass.

Traces

I have always had a vivid imagination. One of my fondest memories as a child was when the eight of us piled into the old Lafayette to go to our grandparents' farm, the Jones County Fair, or some other destination. Because I was second to the youngest, I usually got our mother's lap in the front seat and could see the road and ditch glide along beside us. Jerry, my imaginary mouse (probably from the Tom and Jerry series in the early forties), rode his pony beside the car and jumped twigs and rocks along the way. I didn't realize that my way of encouraging him was by fidgeting continuously until one day I heard in the background noise my mom asking my dad if they should take me to Doctor Sigworth because of the shaking. After that, I tried to consciously control myself, but Jerry continued to ride alongside the car. To this day, when I'm riding along as a passenger, I sometimes glance down to see if he's there, and he always is, but nowadays he rides a Harley.

I think part of my imagination developed the way it did because of my brother Michael. Michael Edward was the sixth child in the family, but he was stillborn. He was the baby who came before me. As I was growing up,

I became more and more aware of his presence, maybe because our mother occasionally reminded us of our two brothers who were already in heaven, and maybe because we often visited the grave where he was buried in the local cemetery. And maybe because I felt I had somehow taken his place on earth. Our older brother, Victor William, who was also stillborn, was buried in another cemetery with our grandparents several miles away, so I didn't think of him so often, but I always felt I shared a special bond with my sister Barbara, who was the next child born after Victor.

Whatever the influences, I felt at a young age the presence of the spiritual and often pictured my guardian angel walking beside me. As I grew older, I seemed to grow in looking for signs in nature, not necessarily spiritual signs but fleeting shapes that are easily missed. I think my love of crocheting helps me see patterns emerging. My grandson Trent seems to have a natural gift for such spotting. When he was five or six, he called me into the living room to see the shapes the sunlight was making on the floor. "Look, Grandma, there's a 'V,' and over there is a 'C'!" He saw in the clouds a variety of shapes and would always point them out to me, "Grandma, there's a cloud bird!" "Grandma, there's a fish cloud!"

Shapes in nature and unusual happenings swim along in my memories of how the visible and invisible interact in our lives. My nephew Peter Erpenbach, born with

Werdnig-Hoffmann disease, a neuro-muscular condition, died in 1987 at the tender age of seven months. The disease caused all his muscles to atrophy except the facial muscles, so he was always smiling, which was part of the reason he got the nickname "Peter Pancake." He was a beautiful child who brought much love to his family and extended family although his presence was all too brief.

In the fall of '87, I went to St. Louis, where his family lived, to a teaching conference at the Hyatt Regency in the center of the city. It was a wonderful opportunity to spend some time with my sister-in-law Val and Peter's two brothers, Gus and Ike. We made arrangements to meet outside the hotel, but since we were going to her home to visit, and since I had to be back for a meeting a few hours later, I said I would follow her in my car. I checked out of the parking garage and drove to where I thought Val was, but she wasn't there. Confused, I started driving around blocks, unaware that I was going away from the hotel. I kept driving and driving, hoping I would see Val's van parked along the curb, waiting for me. After several minutes of driving in the maze that is downtown St. Louis, I found myself crossing a bridge into Illinois! I took the first exit, headed back to the city, pulled over to the side of the street, and pondered what I should do next. It was an age before cell phones and GPS were widespread, and I had neither. I worried about Val worrying about me and what may have happened. Then I suddenly felt reassured. I said a prayer to Peter Pancake to help me find his mom, and the first thought that came into my head was "Go in exactly the opposite direction you think you should go." It seemed ludicrous, but instead of taking a left at the next corner, which felt to me the exact way I should go, I took a right, and after about six blocks, the buildings and streets started looking more familiar. Before long, I sighted the Hyatt, and there was Val's van! I jumped out to explain to her and her then sleeping children my long absence. Apparently, the exit door for the parking ramp was on the other side of the building, and I had become totally turned around in the process. After that incident, whenever I feel lost, my first impulse is to call on Peter Pancake.

Although over the years I occasionally noticed some interesting natural shapes and coincidences, it was not until my sister RoseAnn died in 2001 that I seem to have become much more sensitive to the synchronicity that sometimes happens in ordinary events and in nature that reminds me of the presence of the spiritual. The day after RoseAnn's death, my sister JoAn and I went to a store to buy some silk roses for people to wear at the funeral. We got a big assortment of all different colors, but we couldn't find any red roses, RoseAnn's favorites. Amazingly, when we turned back to go down an aisle we had just come up, there was a beautiful red rose lying on the floor. We got it for our mother to wear. We told RoseAnn's husband, Ivan, about it when we returned to their home, and he cried. Then, as he opened the day's mail, there was a letter from a religious group, asking for money, and enclosed was a card with a quote from S. Therese, the Little Flower: "I will send you roses from Heaven."

That summer, on our drive home from South Dakota after two nieces' graduations in June of that year, I saw the most beautiful rose cloud in the sky. I had been thinking of RoseAnn and missing her so, and the cloud was such a beautiful pink color and seemed to come with us all the way through Minnesota. I just stared at it. It was so unusual. All the other clouds in the sky changed, but it didn't. It just stayed there until the sun was completely down.

My mother told me some time after RoseAnn's death that in her deep sorrow over RoseAnn's suffering, she couldn't cry. She sometimes got beyond tears, where the grief was so deep that she couldn't weep, but she said that after we had called to tell her about RoseAnn's death, one tear came from her blind eye. My mom had been blind in that eye for a number of years. I told her that as RoseAnn was dying, one tear came from the prosthesis in her left eye, the eye that had been removed three years earlier as a result of a cancerous growth. I didn't know that tears could come from a prosthesis. When Mom told me she had a tear from her blind eye, I saw a link in their tears even though they were physically separated by 300 miles. The tears seemed to be not only a sign of their great love for each other, their togetherness in RoseAnn's leaving, but also a sign of the life that goes on even after death, tears coming from eyes that no longer functioned on earth.

On the twenty-ninth anniversary of our Dad's death, June 4, 2001, the year RoseAnn died, I had film I wanted to get developed in my old camera and a few shots left on the roll. I took pictures of various flowers that were blooming in our gardens and then decided to take a picture of the rose I had brought home from RoseAnn's casket. It was black and dead by then, but when I got the pictures back after developing, it looked like it was fresh and alive. There may be some natural explanation, but for me, it was another gift from RoseAnn; although her body had died, she lives on in heaven and in our hearts and our memories.

When RoseAnn was dying, I told her our son was being married on June 16, and we would be thinking of her. RoseAnn loved weddings so much, and she told me she would be there although it was clear to us both that she would not be there physically. The week before the wedding, it rained every day, and on the early morning of the day itself, there was still a mist. The wedding reception was to be held in an outdoor tent on our front lawn, and not long into the morning hours, the sun was shining, and the weather could not have been more beautiful. In the late afternoon when the festivities were winding down, a strong wind blew through from nowhere, and the sky turned very dark, but it didn't rain. My mother, who felt RoseAnn's presence as much or more than I, told me it was RoseAnn letting us know she was in charge of the weather and that it was time for people to go home. After everyone left, a most beautiful rainbow formed out over the lake. The newlyweds stood under it, and we took pictures. It was such a lovely symbol of hope in so many ways, and I knew that on some level RoseAnn was there, at our son's wedding as she had promised.

Because of her gifts with the climate, RoseAnn quickly became my patron saint for weather. One time, a colleague and I were driving en route to a conference when the sky suddenly became dark and foreboding. "Time to pray to RoseAnn," I said, and while the dark sky and lightening seemed to surround us, we arrived safely without going through a drop of rain while other conference attendees came in drenched. Later, my colleague, who became president of a college, told me that whenever weather was an issue, she always prayed to my sister RoseAnn, and her prayers were always answered.

In January of 2010, I was returning home after spending a week with my mother in Iowa. There had been an ice storm the night before, and the trees in Wisconsin were sparkling in the bright morning sunlight. The roads were clear, and I was enjoying the natural beauty and thinking of where I might pull over and take a picture when I missed the sign for a sharp curve to the right in the highway. I started going onto the shoulder, but there was ice, and in trying to correct, I turned too far. All of a sudden, I felt the car spinning out of control. Instead of panic, I felt unnaturally calm. I said to myself, "Oh dear, this is not good. RoseAnn, I need some help here." When the spinning and the tumult finally stopped, I realized I was hanging by my seatbelt, the car upside down in several feet of snow. A driver behind me stopped and ran down into the snow-filled ditch to tell me he had called 911 and help was on the way. It wasn't long before sirens and flashing lights were on the hill above me. The firefighters spoke encouragement while they had me turn my head enough so they could use a giant claw to take off the driver's side front door. Then they cut the seat belt, lowered me onto a stretcher and carried me out of the ditch and up the hill to the waiting ambulance where the EMTs ran some tests and did an assessment. Miraculously, a small bruise on my leg was my only injury. A policeman brought me into the nearest town, where my son Michael met me and took me to meet my husband, Pat. Michael, who is a used-car sales manager, managed to get us a new car over night, and when I first got into the driver's seat, I noticed a silver pin on the visor, a gift from our Michael, who is named after my brother Michael and the Archangel Michael. It is an angel with a banner that reads, "Never drive faster than your guardian angel can fly."

Just four months later, in May of 2010, our mother became very weak, and it was clear that at 104 years of age, she was ready to move on. She was still in her own home, and hospice was called when she could no longer walk. On Mother's Day weekend, when death was near, many family members and friends came; she was so glad to see them and conscious to the end. Mother had said that she was waiting for RoseAnn to come with a rainbow to take her home, and on the day before she died, a beautiful rainbow appeared after a short rain. My sister JoAn, her daughters Vicki and Cristi, and RoseAnn's daughter, Angie, were all there to witness it, and the photo we took looks like the silhouette of a woman carrying the rainbow. It was May 7th, the feast of St. Rose Venerini. On the next day, the feast of St. Victor Maurus (our dad's name was Victor), our mother died, surrounded by family and friends singing "Amazing Grace."

After our mother's death in 2010, it seemed like there were many signs of her continual presence and blessing. After we returned home from the funeral, Pat and I went down to the beach at our home, and there, sitting in a tree overlooking a small river inlet was a beautiful bald eagle. We had never seen one that close, and we had never seen one at the lake in our fifteen years there. I thought immediately of the closing hymn for mom's funeral—"I Will Raise You Up On Eagle's Wings."

Shortly after that, a swan and a family of cranes rested on our shore, something we likewise hadn't seen before. It was like a special gift from our mother, who loved birds so much.

Mom seemed especially helpful that summer after her death with Trent's wooden airplane. Trent had made a papier-mâché Big Bird for her when she came home from the hospital after her surgery in 2009, and Grandma Knight loved it! In summer 2010, Trent was flying his new airplane, and it disappeared into the neighbor's yard. We looked and looked, and then I suggested we say a prayer to Grandma Knight to help us find it. Then Trent noticed the branches of a tree in the neighbor's yard blowing, even though there seemed to be no wind. "Lo and behold," as Great Grandma Knight would always say, the plane flew down from the branches.

On August 6, 2010, when my sister Barbara turned 75, she also experienced our mother's presence. On that day, she and her husband, Kermit, visited our mother's grave. Barbara said that there were some artificial lilacs that our sister JoAn had put on the grave, and they had fallen over, so Barbara started to straighten them out, and there was a baby rabbit under the flowers. As it hopped away, it seemed like a special birthday gift for Barbara.

Our mother loved blue morning glories and had them in her yard every summer. At her funeral, Barbara and Kermit's son Randy, who was very devoted to her, brought packages of morning glory seeds to distribute to everyone who was there. Barb later wrote to me in an email, "I was so surprised last Sunday when I looked at my morning glory trellis. There were blue morning glories blooming. They were growing up the side over the wild purple ones. They came across the top of the trellis and down the other side. I have really been surprised because they stay open all day. During the summer I thought they would just bloom in the morning, but these are blooming all day, and they are so pretty. I think it is a sign from mom!"

During those years, our youngest brother, Keith, was in need of a kidney transplant. The year our mother died, I went to Mayo clinic for tests to see if I could donate one of mine, but it was determined that I wasn't a good candidate. Then on Mother's Day, the first anniversary of our mother's death, the feast of St. Victor Maurus, a kidney became available, and our brother was the recipient. Eight years later, he is doing very well.

My husband and I cared for his aging mother, Laverne, periodically until her death in February of 2015. I was always amazed at her memory while we were caring for her. Whenever I needed to find something in the large house with many closets, a large basement, a furnished front porch, three bedrooms with chests, etc., she seemed to know exactly where the item was. I never gave it much thought until March of that year when we were getting ready to take our grandson Trent to Mexico to spend some time with Pat's brother, his wife, and son. We had obtained Trent's passport and sent it to his mom, but when we went to pick up Trent for our trip, scheduled the following day, the passport was nowhere to be found. Kim, Trent's mom, looked for it in the place where she thought she had put it, but it wasn't there.

So began the exhaustive search to find the passport. Kim, Brent (Kim's husband), Trent, Pat and I went through what seemed like every inch of the house, but when I had given up on possibilities and was standing in the kitchen wondering if it's possible to replace a passport in less than twenty-four hours, Pat's mom came suddenly to my mind, and I said a quick prayer, "Laverne, you always knew where everything is. Where is the passport?" Immediately, my eyes were directed to a narrow pocket hanger in the corner by a cabinet with recipes and notes in it. I took it down, and there behind a bill was the passport! From that moment on, Laverne became my patron saint for lost things. As I grow older, I use her help a great deal, and it seems like she always comes through in one way or another. Recently,

Pat was looking for a quote he needed for his latest book. I couldn't be much help to him in finding it, but I reminded him that his mom always seems to answer our prayers when we can't find something, so I prayed to her. A few days later, he found the quote, not in the source he had seen it in originally, but in an entirely different place.

Whether mere coincidences or gifts from beyond, I am comforted by assurance of the latter. A recent incident, unexplained but so appropriate in retrospect, seemed like a very personal gift. December 16, 2017, was the day of RoseAnn's oldest granddaughter's wedding. Although it had been a strange winter, with frozen days and not much sun, the day of the wedding could not have been more beautiful, even in Iowa. It was bright, sunny, in the 50's, unusually warm. The next day was dark, cold, and dreary, but the wedding day itself had perfect weather.

Pat and I were staying at the Double Tree, a motel in downtown Cedar Rapids. I got up in the early morning, when the sun was just up, to use the bathroom. When I came out of the bathroom, there were two circles of light spots dancing on the floor. I had never seen anything like it before, and I looked for light to be reflecting off the ceiling through a crack in the window curtains. But there were no lights on the ceiling nor any signs the light was reflecting off of anything. Pat was still asleep, and I wondered if the building could be swaying and somehow catching rays of light since we were on the 8th floor, but I could find no explanation. It was lovely, and I just thought it was strange until I pondered it later and thought about RoseAnn and how she would be dancing in heaven on her granddaughter's wedding day and with us in spirit. At the wedding dance itself, my brother, his wife, two nieces and I formed a circle to dance together, but I'm convinced now that spirits were also dancing with us.

I, like everyone I know, have gone through periods of great darkness, of deep sadness. I have sometimes felt crushed by the violence, cruelty, hatred, innocent suffering, and injustices that surround us. I have witnessed and at times shared the brokenness and despair others have experienced. Sometimes, it is very difficult, as Seamus Heaney says in *The Cure at Troy*, to "believe that a further shore is reachable from here," but that belief is not only what keeps me going but also convinced that we can create a much better world if only we can see through the eyes of the spirit.

It may seem a long distance from Jerry riding his pony alongside our old Lafayette, to spirits dancing in circles at my niece's wedding, to eagle's wings "bear[ing] you on the breath of dawn," but the linking of the intangible and the tangible, the visible and the invisible, the spiritual and the bodily is what creates and nourishes the patterns of our lives. Like lace, the fragile threads of our lives reveal forces brought together from the seen and unseen that are both unique for each of us and part of a larger tapestry of human existence, all begun when God breathed over the "empty" and "formless" earth.

A Confused Woman

I gather my book bag, laptop, and purse from the back seat, slam the car door and head up the steps of our faded blue and white Milwaukee bungalow. The mailbox is bulging with envelopes, and a package sits under it. I unlock the front door, go in, deposit my bags and purse on the couch, go back out, gather the package and mail and lock the front door behind me as usual. All the time, I'm singing, "Too-ra-loo-ra-loo-ral, Too-ra-loo-ra-li, Too-ra-loo-ra-loo-ral, hush now, don't you cry! Too-ra-loo-ra-loo-ral, Too-ra-loo-ra-li, Too-ra-loo-ra-loo-ral, that's an Irish lullaby." Don't you hate it when tunes get stuck in your head, and they won't go away? I'd been singing that song for three days since I rocked my six-month-old grandson to sleep.

Once in the living room, I sink into the couch in front of the living room window and start going through the mail, separating it into piles of bills, junk, personal correspondence, flyers, ads, and the package from my brother-in-law. While I'm sorting the mail, a white-haired woman wearing shorts and sneakers comes up the front steps, peering in the window. I glance at her, unsure if she is just dropping off a flyer or coming for some other reason. But as I look again, I see that the woman is still there, going up and down the porch steps. I toss the rest of the mail on the couch and go to the door.

"Hi! What can I do for you?"

The woman begins gesturing and glancing all around her, but she doesn't say anything.

It occurs to me that maybe the woman is hard of hearing. "It's really hot today!" I say in a louder voice. "You're hot. What can I do for you? Do I know you?"

Still no response. The woman just stands there, her arms going as though she is trying to speak sign language but doesn't know how. I am becoming uncomfortable. My first instinct is always to be of help, but what does this woman want?

"I wonder if you're too warm. You've been walking, and you're too warm. Do you know it's over ninety degrees out today? And the humidity! Would you like a drink of water?"

The woman just stands at the bottom of the stairs, moving her arms back and forth.

"I think you should come inside. How about a glass of cold water? You seem overcome by the heat. Come on in. You can sit and cool down, and I'll get you some cold water."

I go down the steps, take the woman by the arm and lead her up the steps into the house. The woman comes willingly, but once in the house, I realize that it's warm in here, too, so I take the woman into the study, ease her down into the lazy-boy and turn on the window air conditioner.

"Just sit there for a moment, and I'll get you some cold water and a cold cloth for your head. Okay?"

The woman just sits and stares in front of her.

I return with ice water and a wet washcloth. "There, that should help. Now tell me, where do you live?"

For the first time, the woman looks at me. "Here," she says.

Ohhhhh dear, I think. *This is weird. What do I do now?* Part of me wants to burst out laughing—"*Hey, Pat, do you know there's another older woman living in the house with us?*" and the other part is beginning to panic that I may have a real problem on my hands. I'm supposed to leave shortly to go to the lake. Pat is already there, cooking out steaks at our vacation home, and this woman may need more than a glass of cold water. As I glance around the room, I suddenly realize how untidy my husband's study is with stacks of books, unopened letters, a cup with a tea bag tag hanging out. I feel the need to keep talking to try to get this woman back to some kind of reality.

"Wow! That's amazing! Please don't look at the house. It's a real mess. You know what? My next-door neighbor is a nurse. I'm going to call her and ask her to come over and take a look at you. You look really warm. Maybe the heat is making you confused. Is that okay? If I call Judy next door?"

The woman nods—*well, that's something!* I go to the

phone on the desk, thinking that she must be understanding something on some level.

"Judy, hi, it's Phyllis next door. There's a woman here. She came to the front door just after I got home. She may have seen me drive in. I think she's gotten a bit too warm. Could you come over and see if she's all right? . . . Who is she? I'm not sure." I turn to the woman, "Excuse me, can you tell me your name?"

The woman begins gesturing again.

"'Where does she live?'—Judy, she seems to be overcome by the heat, and I don't think she knows for sure. She's not really communicating. Could you come right over? Thanks."

I go over to the chair and reverse the wash cloth on the woman's forehead. "My neighbor Judy's coming right over. She's an RN, and she'll know what to do. Here, let me get that cloth cold again. I'll go open the door for Judy. I'll be right back, okay?"

Judy is coming up the front steps peering into the window as I go to the living room and open the door.

"She just came up and stood at the bottom of the porch, and when I asked her what she wanted, she was trying to tell me something, but I don't know what it was. She doesn't seem to know who she is or where she is." Judy rolls her eyes and goes into the study.

"Hi, I'm next-door Judy. You got a little warm out

there? I'm going to take your temperature. Phyllis, can you get me another cold towel for around her neck?" Judy takes a thermometer out of her pocket. Then to the woman, "Where do you live?"

The woman replies, "Here."

Judy turns to me as I leave to get the towel, "You're right. She's a bit confused—or there's something Pat hasn't told you."

"She seemed to know the house. Do you think she might live in a bungalow?"

"Oh, well, that really narrows it down a lot, Phyllis!" Judy snickers. She eases the woman's mouth open and inserts the thermometer. As I return with the wet washcloth, Judy is taking the thermometer out of the woman's mouth.

"Well, her temperature is about 100, but this is a rectal—it's all I could find." Judy leans very close to the woman's face and asks, "Can you tell me your name?"

The woman gestures but says nothing. Judy looks at me and shrugs: "I think you should probably call 911. She's quite warm and disoriented. Better be on the safe side."

I go to the phone and dial 911 for the first time in my life. "Hi. We have a woman here who seems to be overcome with the heat. The address is 2128 N. 59th Street. Sure, I'll hold—"

Judy rearranges the cloths. "She just turned up at your front door?"

"Well, I did see her walking down the block when I was driving down the street. She looked a little familiar, and then when I came in the house . . ." I'm interrupted by the emergency operator asking, "Will you repeat the emergency?"

After I give the details and hang up the phone, I realize we don't know who to notify that we probably will be taking their wife/mother/sister into the hospital.

Judy reads my mind. "I'll go get Marilyn Schofield. She knows everyone in a six-mile radius."

I get some fresh water for the woman. "Are you feeling any better? Can you drink some more water? I'll be right back."

When I come back to the study, Judy and Marilyn are just walking in. Marilyn doesn't hesitate when she sees the woman.

"Oh sure! It's Mary Murphy! Her son lives on the Circle. I see Mary out walking all the time." Marilyn leans over the woman and speaks loudly, "Hello, Mary. Do you know me? I'm Marilyn Schofield. I live in the duplex on the corner." And then to me, "Sure, it's Mary Murphy."

I am shocked. "Mary Murphy? I know Mary Murphy! This is Mary?"

The woman smiles for the first time, and suddenly it occurs to me why this woman looked familiar. "Oh, Mary, I'm so sorry—I didn't recognize you! I haven't seen you for so long, and you've lost weight! I'm so embarrassed."

I turn to Judy and Marilyn. "You know, I've known Mary Murphy for years! Her husband, Tom, was chair of my department at Marquette when I was there. We all used to belong to St. Sebastian's parish. I can't believe I didn't recognize her, but it's been so long . . . She did look familiar."

Just then the doorbell rings, and two paramedics with kits are waiting. Marilyn has to get home to tend to food on the stove, and the paramedics come in. Judy fills them in, "Hi, I'm an RN from St. Luke's. Her temperature is around 100, but we couldn't get an accurate reading. She's quite confused."

I get out a phone book to look up Mary's home and family numbers. The paramedic takes the woman's blood pressure. "BP 130 over 70."

"*Wow,*" I think, "*that's better than mine usually is. Maybe there's nothing to worry about!*"

The paramedic speaks to the woman, "How are you feeling? Got a little warm, did ya? Can you tell me your name?"

The woman gestures but says nothing.

By this time I am finding some numbers in the phone book. "It's Mary Murphy," I say, "her son lives up on the Circle. I'm trying to find someone to notify."

The paramedic speaks to the woman again. "Your name is Mary?"

The woman nods.

"Mary, can you tell me what day it is?"

The woman nods and appears about to speak but ends up gesturing again with her hands.

The paramedic tries again, "Well, Mary, how about your address? Where do you live?"

The woman answers, "Here."

The paramedic looks at Judy, who shrugs, and then at me.

"I'm not sure what she means by that." Then I speak to the woman, "Mary, I'm sorry I can't remember your children's names. There's a 'Melissa Murphy' here. Is that your daughter?"

The woman nods.

Judy asks, "What's the number, Phyllis? I'll try it." She punches the number into her cellphone.

Meanwhile the paramedic is calling the hospital.

"There's no one at Melissa's house," Judy says, "but she left her cell-phone number. Do you have a pencil, Phyllis?"

Meanwhile the paramedic makes a connection. "Yes, we have a female Caucasian, late sixties—early seventies, elevated temperature, BP normal, otherwise stable, but she's disoriented, may be dehydrated. Do you have any beds?"

My phone rings, and I answer, "Hello . . . No, Mike. Everything's all right. It was Mary Murphy out walking—

she got too hot, so we called 911 . . . No, everything's all right. How did you know the ambulance was here? Oh sure—" I nod to Judy, "Bob down the block saw the ambulance and called Mike at work."

Judy's cellphone rings. "Hi, Lori . . . Yeah. Lots going on at the Careys. You know the people who live on the Circle in the brick house near the corner? . . . No, not the Sherman's, the ones next door? . . . No, the other side . . . on the Circle . . . Yeah, that one. Well, the guy's mom was out walking and got overheated, and Phyllis brought her in and called me. Anyway, they're taking her to the hospital—probably St. Joe's . . . How did you know . . . Bob down the block?"

The paramedic finishes his conversation, "OK, St. Joe's it is." Both paramedics leave to get the gurney. Meanwhile, Judy dials the number for Melissa.

"Hello, Melissa? I'm calling about your mom. She was out walking and got overheated, and she seems to be a little confused. The paramedics are here, and they're going to take her to St. Joe's . . . Mary Murphy . . . Oh, I see . . . Sure, that's great. Thanks a lot."

Judy switches off. "Melissa's not Mary's daughter. She's the ex daughter-in-law, but she said she would try to call her ex to tell him that his mom will be at St. Joe's, but he doesn't always answer his phone."

"Thanks, Judy." The woman is now unbuttoning her

blouse. I stop her and hold her hands. "Oh, Mary, I know you're warm but best leave on the blouse. Listen, I'm going to the hospital with you, Mary. Judy called Melissa, and she's calling your son, and he'll probably be there before we are. Not to worry. Everything is going to be all right."

The paramedics come and put Mary on the gurney, I get my purse, cell phone, lock the door, and board the ambulance in the seat next to the driver, and we're off to Saint Joseph's. It doesn't seem to be an emergency to me, but the driver puts on the siren to get us through the busy streets. People stop, stare, then move on. In fewer than ten minutes, we are pulling into the emergency ramp at St. Joseph's Hospital.

The paramedics unload the gurney. I tell Mary I'll meet her inside and walk down the drive to make a phone call.

When my husband answers, I feel like I'm coming up for air after being submerged in water.

"Pat! You'll never guess what happened. I came home from the workshop and was going to come right up to the lake, but as I was going through the mail, Mary Murphy came up to the door, but she was all confused. She didn't know where she was or who she was . . . Mary Murphy! Yes! I didn't even recognize her. She looked familiar, but I couldn't place her. I haven't seen her since Tom's funeral, and that's been almost a year. She's lost weight, and her hair looks different, but Marilyn Schofield came over, and she recognized her right away. I was so embarrassed . . . I don't know. She's really confused; anyway, they're admitting her—"

Just then a woman in a blue hospital garb comes out with a clipboard and a phone book. "Hold on just a minute."

"There are two Mary Murphy's in our registry. Do you know which one this is?"

"Hmm, let's see. Well, her husband was Tom Murphy. He died just last year, so they still could be listed as Tom and Mary. They live near Washington Boulevard—one of those streets in the 40's."

"1844 N. 49th Street?"

"Yes, that's it, I'm sure."

"Born 08/12/37?"

"That sounds about right."

The woman goes back in the door, and I turn back to my cell. "Sorry about that. Anyway, I'm at St. Joe's, and it's already after 7:00, so I don't know if I'm going to make it there tonight. I want to stay here until one of the children comes . . . Tim? That's her son's name? I couldn't remember any of her children's names! Isn't that awful? I can't believe I didn't even recognize her! We called Melissa, who's married to one of her sons, or who *was* married to one of her sons, and she was going to try to contact him, but nobody's here yet. I can try Tim on the Circle. Why didn't I think of checking addresses? . . . No, Mike's at work.

He called to see what all the excitement was with the ambulance and everything . . . Bob down the block . . . Yes, I came in the ambulance with her. Judy said she'd give me a ride home when I'm ready. Look, I should go in and see what's going on. I'll call you later, okay? Bye, love you."

When I go inside, the emergency room is alive. There is a nurses' desk with a reception area, doctors, nurses, aides, wheel chair patients, a policeman coming in with a wounded man, a maintenance man with a mop and pail—all are moving quickly on their own paths through the area.

The receptionist points me to one in a line of compartments separated by hanging sheets. Mary is sitting on the edge of a bed in a hospital gown; she is already being attached to a monitor by an aide. Her clothes are folded on a chair, her tennis shoes beneath.

I take Mary's hand. "How are you doing, Mary?" I speak to the aide, "How is she doing?"

"The doctor will be in shortly."

"Well, Mary, are you feeling any better? The doctor will check to see if everything is all right, and I'm sure one of your children will be here soon."

Mary nods and plays with her gown.

I think I should try to keep her as alert as possible until the doctor examines her. "Aren't those gowns awful? They really haven't improved them any, have they. Here, let me give you a hand." I check the ties in back and look at the monitor. "Boy, these machines are something, aren't they? All those numbers. I suppose they're measuring pulse and pressure and heart rate. Good thing they don't measure weight! Well, you don't need to worry about that, but I could sure lose a few pounds. I suppose the lower the numbers, the better. Like weight—and blood pressure—seems the lower, the better. And cholesterol. Pat has a cholesterol problem." Mary looks up at me. "You know, my husband, Pat. He eats oatmeal every morning for breakfast, not supposed to eat cheese or ice cream or red meat—the things he loves—or alcohol! Now he's on Lipitor, but that can harm your liver, so he has to go get tests to be sure his liver's all right, and I suppose they'll give him something to counteract the effects of the Lipitor. His mom just fell and got a hairline fracture in her hip, and they put her on morphine for the pain, but then she got so constipated, they had to give her Milk of Magnesia, but that upset her stomach, so they had to give her something for the acid, or maybe that's what the Milk of Magnesia was for. No, I think that was for the gas . . . And then you see those ads on television—you know like for Lunesta. It's supposed to make you sleep, but the side effects are worse than staying awake all night, 'Stop usage if you experience suicidal thoughts, or if you develop constipation, diarrhea, or a sudden urge to beat up your next-door neighbor'—well you know what I mean. You know what our neighbor said the other day? He used to be a pharmaceutical salesman, and he said that he thinks all these people being diagnosed with diabetes and high cholesterol and high blood pressure—that it's just the drug companies lowering what numbers are acceptable, so they can sell more drugs."

Mary seems even more confused. "Sorry, I got carried away there. How are you doing?"

Mary looks at her clothes on the chair and starts sliding off the edge of the bed.

I take her hands and look into her face. "No, Mary, you can't leave now. The doctor will be here in a minute, and your son—oh, Pat remembered your son's name on the Circle—Tim! Was he married to Melissa?"

Mary nods.

"Melissa said she'd call her husband—I mean Tim—so he should be here soon."

Just then the doctor enters the cubicle and starts examining Mary.

"Hello, Mary. I'm Doctor Sharif."

I decide it's a good time to try to reach Tim. "Mary, I'll be right back." I step outside the cubicle, look in the phone book, and dial the number. No answer, but an answering machine where I leave my message. "Hello, Tim. This is Phyllis Carey from 59th Street. I don't know if Melissa got in touch with you, but your mom was out walking and got a bit over-heated. She stopped at our house, and my neighbor, who's a nurse, thought we should call 911, and they thought we should bring her to St. Joe's. The doctor's looking at her now, but she's a bit confused and wants to leave, so if you could come to St. Joe's, it would be great. She's all right—just over-heated and a bit confused. If you could come over, I'm sure it would be a comfort for her to see one of the children. Thanks!"

When I return to the cubicle, the doctor has finished the physical exam and is asking Mary questions.

"Mary, can you tell me your birthday?"

Mary smiles for the second time.

I remember the birth date the receptionist mentioned. "Mary, don't you have a birthday coming up?"

Mary nods.

"Isn't it in August?"

Mary nods.

"Around the 12th or 13th?"

The doctor interrupts, "Please, do you mind? I'm trying to see how coherent she is." He speaks to Mary, "Mary, do you know what day of the week it is?"

Mary smiles.

The doctor turns to me, "Do you know this woman? Is she usually more alert?"

"Oh, yes. Mary's a very well-educated woman. She's very articulate. This isn't at all what she's normally like. She has a wonderful sense of humor. She knows a lot about—"

The doctor interrupts me, "Has she spoken to you at all today?"

"Well, she said she lived at my house two or three times. Actually, she said 'Here' when we asked her where she lived. I don't know why she said that."

"Has she ever worked outside the home?"

"Oh, yes. You worked at Sojourner Truth House, didn't you, Mary? I think she stopped about five years ago, but she's always helping with the grandchildren, and she probably does other volunteer work. Do you think she's just dehydrated? Do you know what's going on with her?"

"We need to run a few tests. I'm going to order a cranial CT scan." The doctor leaves the cubicle.

"Mary, it's going to be fine. They're going to do some more tests, but everything will be fine."

Mary starts sliding out of bed again. "No, Mary, you can't go yet. They're going to do more tests." Mary looks at me and begins to cry. She moans and rocks back and forth.

I sit on the bed and put my arm around her. "Oh, Mary, I know how hard it must be. It's been a really hard day for you. And I know it's been hard without Tom. He was such a wonderful man. But Mary, he's watching over you now. He'll take care of everything. Not to worry. Oh, don't cry . . . although they say crying is good for you, and if you have tears, that must mean the water is coming back into your system, doesn't it?"

I try to think happier thoughts. "Oh, did I tell you that our Brian graduated from Lakeshore Tech! We are so happy for him and so proud! He's an electrical technical engineer. No, he's an electrical mechanical technician, I think. Anyway, he's going to Silver Lake now to get a bachelor's degree in electrical mechanical engineering or something like that. And our Michael! He went to UWM, but he's not sure what he's going to do, so now he's working at the Vehicle Emissions testing place in the morning and at Chi-Chi's El Pronto at night. He can't decide if he wants to be a race car driver or a chef. Don't they grow up fast?"

Mary continues to sob and to try to move out of the bed. "Oh, Mary, now you know you can't go yet. They'll be right here for those tests. I wish you weren't so sad. It has to be a bit scary, I know. You know, my sister RoseAnn died a year ago last spring, and I still miss her so much. I wanted to thank you for the lovely note you wrote. It meant so much to me. Here you were, mourning your own Tom, and reaching out to me to give me comfort when RoseAnn died. She was such a wonderful person. You would have really liked her. She started her own business to help the elderly. She was even on the board of the Alzheimer's Association in Omaha. She knew everything older people need. Our whole family walks in the Alzheimer's walk every year just because of RoseAnn—We were so close."

Mary seems calmer. I decide to continue. "RoseAnn and I were very close. She used to play practical jokes on me. One time we went to our Grandma's house for an overnight. I loved going there because my Grandma had the softest blankets in the world. I think they were stuffed with goose down. You felt like you were sleeping on a cloud. Anyway, we weren't in bed for five minutes, and RoseAnn started coughing, and then she started sneezing. Her face got really red, and she got short of breath. My Grandma came when she heard the noise and said that RoseAnn must be allergic to the goose down. Anyway, Grandma phoned our dad, and he came and took us home. I was so mad at RoseAnn, but then she told me the next morning that she had faked it all because she was homesick. I couldn't believe it." Only an occasional sob is coming from Mary.

I take that as a sign I should continue. "Then, there was the time RoseAnn told my sisters and me that Dad used to write her special notes and put them in her lunch sack. We didn't get any notes, and we all idolized my Dad. Then when she was dying, she told me to email my sisters when she was gone to tell them that it was clear that Dad loved her best because she was the first of the girls to go to heaven to be with him." I am beginning to feel very sad, so I pull up another memory. "We used to sleep together when we were growing up—but she always took all the covers, and she loved to sing herself to sleep . . . 'Too-ra-loo-ra-loo-ral, Too-ra-loo-ra-li.' My sister JoAn and I sang it to her when she was dying." I hear the song in my head, and a new wave of sadness washes over me. I feel the tears starting to swell in my eyes, but Mary is starting to nod with fatigue. I reach for the Kleenex and wipe my eyes.

"Maybe you should get some rest, Mary," I say, while lifting her legs so that she can lie on the bed. I cover her with a sheet. I think of the loneliness she must feel with Tom gone, and the sadness of our family and RoseAnn's family with her presence no longer in our lives. Mary is stirring and trying to sit up. I sit on the bed and continue with my monologue.

"Now Mary, I know you can feel Tom's presence at times, and actually, RoseAnn is still here in many ways. Here . . ." I feel the echo in the word that Mary spoke when I asked her where she lived. "RoseAnn's great with the weather! I have a friend who always prays to RoseAnn when she has a weather problem. When Brian and Kim got married last summer, I told RoseAnn she was in charge of the weather. We planned to have an outside reception. Well, it was very rainy in the week ahead of the wedding, but the day of the wedding was perfect, and in the evening, she sent a small wind storm and the most gorgeous rainbow! We thought it was RoseAnn's special gift for the newlyweds." Mary becomes alert and glances around the cubicle. She looks like she may start crying again.

"Well, that's enough of that! Say, now that I think of it, Kathleen Scullin said she had lunch with you a few weeks ago. She said she had a wonderful time. She's a great person, isn't she? Did you know that we are co-chairing the English Department together? We call ourselves 'co-dependents.' Actually, we're really a great team. She's a wonderful cook, too. We celebrate birthdays in the department, and she brought a 'death by chocolate' pie that was to die for . . . Well, I guess that's redundant—and a bit morbid as well."

"Uh, Mary, now Mary, don't worry about the CT Scan. I've never had one, but I don't think they're that bad. That term—CT scan—reminds me of a funny story. Actually, you know my next-door neighbor, Judy, who took your temperature? Well, they had a rabbit named Carrots. That rabbit must have been 18 years old, and her husband, John—I mean Judy's husband—I don't know if Carrots was a male or female, and animals don't get married anyway, at least not yet. Excuse me, I think I'm getting giddy. Anyway, John was very devoted to that rabbit, and when it got really sick, he took it to the animal E.R., and the vet wanted to give it a CT scan. Judy's very funny, and she wasn't overly fond of that rabbit, so when John called her to ask if the vet should do the CT scan, Judy said, 'No.' So John said they wanted to know if they should give Carrots artificial respiration in case things got bad. Judy told him just to have them call her at work, and when she got home, she would do it herself. She's a nurse, you know. Teaches CPR." I start chuckling as I always do when I tell that story. Just then an aide comes in with a wheel chair to take Mary for the CT scan.

I'm laughing and wiping my eyes. "We were just reminiscing." I say to the aide. "Don't worry, Mary. It won't hurt, and I'll be here when you get back."

While Mary goes to get the CT scan, I step out the Emergency Room door to call Judy.

"Judy, it's Phyllis. No, I'm not ready to come home yet. They just took Mary up for a CT scan, but I can't understand why none of the kids are here yet . . . No. Nobody . . . Do you think you could walk up to the Circle to see if Tim's home? . . . Yeah, his name is Tim. Pat remembered it. Maybe he hasn't checked voice messages . . . Thanks, Judy. I'll let you know when I'm ready to come home. I think I'll try Mary's house to see if any of the kids are there."

I dial Mary Murphy's home phone, and a woman answers.

"Hello? Who is this?—Mary? (*pause)* No, did you say Mary? Is—that—*you*, Mary? Well, but, Mary, it's so good to hear your voice! But who is that woman? Oh, I'm so sorry. I mean I'm really sorry. This is Phyllis Carey. I have a woman here, and I thought it was you. I mean, I'm at St. Joe's, and there was this woman who came to our house, and she was overcome with the heat, and the lady across the street said it was you, and so we came to the hospital, and the woman is getting a CT scan, but I told everyone it was you, and the lady said she was you. Well, she didn't exactly say that, but she nodded when they asked her if her name was Mary Murphy . . . Oh, the hospital called? Well, they did say there were two Mary Murphy's. Now they must think she's the other one! Oh, dear! And I left messages on Tim's home phone and cell phone . . . He's there with you? Oh, I'm so sorry. Please tell him I'm so sorry. I must have really upset your family. But I'm so glad you're all right! . . . Yes, the kids are fine. Brian just graduated—oh I'd better not go into that right now. I've got to go back to tell them that woman isn't you, but now I don't know who she is. Oh, Lordy—sure, I'll call you when I find out. Listen, Mary, I'm really sorry about all of this, and I so appreciated the card you sent when my sister RoseAnn died—I know, it's so hard—Oh, no, Mary, I didn't know you've been having heart problems. I'm so sorry. Can they do anything about it?—Oh dear. Yes, I'll definitely pray—Yes, I'll let you know. Talk to you later. Bye."

I am in shock. I mean shock. I think I need medical attention myself. What the hell is going on? Who the hell is that woman? Why the hell am I here at St. Joe's?

I call Pat, "Pat, you're not going to believe this! That woman isn't Mary Murphy . . . Yes, I know Mary Murphy, and I thought the woman must be her and that I just didn't recognize her . . . Well, Marilyn was so sure, and I haven't seen Mary for at least a year, and she looked so familiar, and she nodded when they called her that . . . *You're* embarrassed? Listen, I have to go back in and tell them at the desk. Oh, Lordy . . . I'll call you later."

I call Judy. "Judy, it's Phyllis. I don't know how to tell you this, but the woman I brought to the hospital is NOT Mary Murphy . . . I just talked to Mary. I mean the REAL Mary. I thought I would call her home to see if any of the kids had gone over there, and SHE answered the phone . . . No, Tim wasn't home because he's over with Mary . . . He got the message, and called his mom, and then they called the hospital to tell them Mary Murphy wasn't there, but the hospital must have thought it was the other Mary Murphy because I had told them this woman was Mary Murphy . . . No, I have no idea who she is . . . Do you think we should ask Marilyn Schofield if she looks like someone else? No, forget it . . . Well, I'll stay here until she comes back from the tests. Maybe the hospital can figure out who she is . . . Sure. Thanks, Judy."

I walk back into the emergency room entrance and approach the desk. Lots of activity is going on, and no one pays any attention to me. Finally, I lean on the counter, and a nurse's aide working on the computer looks up.

"Can I help you?"

"You know the woman I brought here?"

She checks the chart. "The one in number 8? Let's see—Mary Murphy?"

"Yes. I mean, no. I mean the woman that was in there was the woman I brought, but she isn't Mary Murphy."

"Then who is she?"

"I have no idea."

"Wait a minute. You brought a woman to the E.R., and you don't know who she is?"

"No. I mean, yes, I brought her here, but I don't know who she is. I thought I knew her. I mean, I thought she was a woman I know, but I just talked to *that* woman on the phone, so now I have no clue who *this* woman is."

Doctor Sharif, who has been half listening to our conversation comes over to the counter, and other nurses and nurses' aides start to gather.

The nurse's aide speaks to the group, "The woman in number 8 is a Jane Doe."

The doctor looks at her and then at me and then at her and then at me. "But you told me she was a well-educated woman. You were trying to tell me when her birthday was."

"I'm sorry. I thought I knew this woman. She came to my door, and she looked familiar, and the neighbor was sure it was Mary Murphy, but when I called her home to see if any of her children might be there, Mary Murphy answered the phone! I know it's confusing—I'm confused—but the bottom line is that this woman is not

Mary Murphy. I don't know who she is. Where did she come from? How are we going to find out? She could be anyone!"

The nurse's aide dials the phone as another aide comes around the corner with the woman, a.k.a Mary Murphy, in a wheelchair back from the C-T scan. "Well, we'll start with the Milwaukee Police Department and see if there are any reports of missing persons. By the way, Dr. Carey, I had you for a literature course."

Now I think I have really lost it. "Pardon me?"

The nurse's aide replies, "I had you for a class. I recognized you when you came in. About 10 years ago—*Women Writers*, I think it was."

I try to regain my professional calm while glancing at the aide's name tag. "Oh, of course . . . I thought you looked familiar! Jennifer Chadwick, of course!"

"Actually, I was Jennifer Olson when I was in college." She speaks into the phone, "Hello. This is St. Joe's emergency room. We have a Jane Doe here—white, late sixties-early seventies—seems to have had a heat stroke. Any missing persons matching that description?"

"Jennifer Olson . . . of course. What a day!"

The aide, a.k.a. Jennifer, hangs up the phone, "No one matching that description has been reported to the Milwaukee Police Department at this time, but they'll send some people over."

"That's a good idea, Jennifer. Mary—I mean the lady—she's back now. I think I'll go talk to her."

I go back into the cubicle. Mary, that is, the woman, is lying in bed, plucking at her hospital nightgown.

"Hello there, how was the CT Scan? How are you feeling?"

The woman nods faintly. She seems very sleepy.

"Oh, I know you must be exhausted. It's been quite a day, hasn't it? Quite a day! Well, I feel as though we've gotten to know each other a bit. Or at least you got to know quite a bit about me anyway. Although I guess I just babbled a lot, but you're a really good listener."

The woman nods faintly.

"Well, I think I'm going to leave now and let you get some sleep. Is that all right with you?"

The woman nods again faintly.

"I'll be back first thing in the morning. You get a good night's sleep, okay?" As I start to leave, a sudden thought occurs to me. "By the way, what did you say your name was?"

"Peg."

"Peg? Did you say Peg??"

The woman nods again faintly.

"And what was your last name, again, Peg?

The woman smiles.

"Well, I guess I'll see you tomorrow, Peg."

I go back to the nurse's station. "Jennifer, she told me her name was Peg, but I couldn't get a last name."

Jennifer grabs a pad. "I'll try."

I can see Jennifer talking to the woman through the slightly open sheets of the cubicle. Meanwhile, Dr. Sharif comes out of a cubicle, looks briefly at me as though he is about to say something and then just shakes his head and walks on. A policeman comes by with a wounded man in shackles. I suddenly feel totally exhausted.

Jennifer returns to the station. "I got something. She said it was Dels or Pells–strange name, if it's really hers."

I look in the phone book on the counter. "Hmmm, No Dels—there's Del Rosso and Delsman. Let me try Pells. Wait, there's a J. Pels on 72nd and North. That's not that far from where we live. Do you think we should call and see . . . ?"

Jennifer lifts her hand as though she is about to respond in class. "I think it's probably best to wait for the police. We're not even sure that's her name . . . Why don't you go home, Dr. Carey. You look really tired. You did right in bringing her here. The police can take it from here. Go home and get a good night's sleep."

I look at my watch. It is now 9:30. I've been here since 5:00. "Yes, I think I will. I told her I'd be back first thing in the morning, so I'll come back to see how she's doing. Hope they can figure out who she is by then . . . Thanks so much for all your help, Jennifer!"

I dial Judy. "Hello, Judy. I'm ready to come home now . . . What group home? I didn't even know there was a group home on 59th and Vine. No one's missing? Gee, I never even thought of that. I wonder if the police will check with other group homes? Do you think I should go back and ask the Nurse's Aide to suggest it? . . . Yeah, you're right. Come and get me—someone needs to come and get me. Thanks, Judy."

Once home, I call Pat. "Hi, it's me again . . . No, we don't know for sure who she is. When I went to tell her I was leaving for the night, I asked her what her name was, and she said 'Peg,' and the nurse got some sort of last name out of her, but we're not sure. I'll come to the lake tomorrow after I go see her again. Did you know there's a group home on 59th and Vine? . . . I didn't know that. Anyway, Judy walked down there, but no one's missing . . . I'm so exhausted. I'll call you first thing in the morning."

I fall on the couch with the half-sorted mail and package. Then I get up, go to the kitchen and pour myself a glass of wine. Then back to the couch. Just then my cell phone rings.

"Hello . . . On the news? Wait, I've got to get a pencil."

I dig a pen out of my purse and grab an envelope from the mail. "They said she was from out of town? Visiting where?—But West Allis—that's quite a ways from our house . . . Mild dementia? . . . Margaret F-e-l-l-s? . . . I'd better call that police number. I'll call you back later."

"Hello. My husband in Manitowoc called to say there was a missing woman on the ten o'clock news. I mean, that the West Allis police are looking for a missing woman who was visiting family from out of town. I mean . . . What I'm trying to say is I brought a woman to the Emergency Room at St. Joseph's Hospital late this afternoon, and I think she's the missing woman you're looking for. She gave us a name at the end of the night, and it sounds like the right person . . . You'll call the E.R. at St. Joe's? . . . Thank you so much . . . Yes, you're welcome."

I sit back on the couch and take a sip of wine. What a mixed-up day! What must Mary Murphy think of me? And that poor woman? I jabbered like an idiot most of the time I was with her.

I sit in silence for a few moments and then start thumbing through the mail on the couch again as I had earlier in the day. The package catches my eye. "Ah, RoseAnn, how I miss you. You would have known exactly what to do today. And what has your husband sent me?

"Well, how about that! Ivan thought I might like to have your personal copy of *A Caregiver's Guide to Alzheimer's Disease: 300 Tips for Making Life Easier.* Are you kidding me? Did you think you had to motivate me to read this book!"

I begin to see connections and start to smile. "You always worried so much about older people! Did you decide to start your own business up there? *Celestial Dementia Entrepreneurship*? Well, you certainly have a lot of kinks to work out! I think I'd start with a better communications system—or better screening for your workers—maybe choose someone who already knows something about the job? Talk about customer service! That poor woman was so lost. What can it be like to be that lost? And she was afraid. She must have been so afraid. And confused. So confused. Well, that made two of us. And me going on and on. She just came out of nowhere—a stranger I thought I knew. But you made sure she got some help. Never mind the quality. You were here today, weren't you? Here. You're still *here* . . .

I raise my glass: *"Here!"*

Treasures

When our second and third grandchildren were toddlers—Alexander Brian, born 9/15/2010 and Sophia Loren, born 11/20/2013—I didn't have the opportunity to babysit them as I had for Trent. But our bonds grew stronger as they grew, and watching their interaction with one another and with Trent was and is a source of great joy. One time when Alex was still a baby and getting a lot of attention, Trent, aged seven or eight, asked, "Grandma, do you like me more than Alex?" "Teachable moment" sprang up in my mind. Also a glimpse of the possible real question behind the one just asked.

"Well, Trent, do you ever wonder if people like Alex better than they like you?"

"Yep," he replied. "Sometimes I do."

"Trent, do you love your mom more than your dad?"

"Not really."

"Do you love your dad more than your mom?"

"No."

"Do you love Grandpa more than me."

"No."

"Do you love me more than Grandpa."

"No."

"So, you see, you can love two people or lots of people in different ways, and it doesn't mean you love someone more than you love someone else." I had been fixing an apple for his lunch and looked at him as I finished the sentence. Trent was sitting, looking quite thoughtful, and then he said, "Grandma, I think I will remember this moment for the rest of my life."

Trent became a wonderful big brother. In fact, he gave me some advice from time to time. Once, when I wanted Alex, a toddler at the time, to come and wash his hands for lunch, Alex was not about to be distracted from his toys. Trent said, "Grandma, that's not the way you do it. You say, 'Alex, don't you dare come and wash your hands. Don't do it!' and he'll come right away."

Of course, as Alex grew, he also gave me advice about Sophia. One day I was reading a story to Sophia, and Alex crawled up in my chair to share the story. Sophia soon wanted her doll and jumped down to get it. When she returned, Alex said, "Grandma, tell her she can't come back." I said to Alex that I couldn't do that, and he replied, "Sure, Grandma, tell her she can't come back, and then she'll start to cry, and then you say, 'All right, you can come back.'"

But Alex usually showed a much more sensitive side, which was endearing. When I was growing up in our little town in Iowa, at family meals we always said grace,

"Bless us, O Lord, and these thy gifts, which we are about to receive, from thy bounty through Christ Our Lord. Amen." When I was a child, we always said grace after meals as well, but that faded at some point, and now all I can remember is "We give thee thanks . . ." although the prayer was equally as short. Now with our informal meals, we no longer say grace, but when family is gathered for some occasion, we always start the meal with grace. At some point, my husband and I added the prayer for the dead, to remember mostly our own parents, siblings, other relatives, and friends who have died, "May the souls of the faithful departed, through the mercy of God, rest in peace. Amen." And, when we moved into our home on the lake, I got into the habit of adding another prayer at the end, "and thank you, God, for bringing [whichever guests, family members, etc. were at our table] into our home."

Our sons no longer say the prayer with us, and two of the three grandchildren are now Lutherans, so they have their own version of grace. The oldest grandchild doesn't belong to any religion, so my husband and I simply pray the grace out loud ourselves when family members are present. One time, then five-year-old Alex spoke up after the grace when I thanked God for bringing him, his dad, and his little sister into our home. He said, "and invisible Trent." Trent wasn't present, but Alex wanted to include him as well. I thought that was a wonderful thought for a five-year-old, and so on occasions after that, when Trent wasn't there and Alex was, I would thank God for bringing everyone who was there into our home and then nod to Alex, and he would add "and invisible Trent."

Then one day, when my husband and I started the grace, a new voice could be heard. Now seven-year-old Alex said all the prayers with us and at the end mouthed to me "invisible Trent." My husband and I (and Alex's dad) were surprised and so pleased that Alex joined us in the grace. He said he had been practicing at home, and knew the prayer by heart, so he could say it himself and join with us in the prayer.

It was truly a moment of grace.

At age eight, Alex began piano lessons, and since no one in his family played the piano, I offered to work with him one day a week after school on his music. It became a fun ritual of meeting him when school dismissed for the day and practicing in a music room at the school for a half hour. Afterwards, we went to Menchie's Frozen Custard for a treat while playing the name game, and then I dropped him off at home.

One day, his "Technique" book directed him to play two octaves with his middle finger on his left hand and then on his right. Alex was clearly embarrassed. I assured him that it was to strengthen that finger, but he seemed to feel it was a naughty thing to do. He smiled all the time he was doing it. Later that day, on the way to the after-piano-treat, he got distracted and forgot we were playing "the name game," as we called it. You think of something and give the first letter as a clue, something like twenty questions. I had chosen "Flintstones," the title of the piece he had been practicing for his upcoming recital. To bring him back to focus, I said without thinking, "Alex, you still haven't thought of the F-word."

"'The F-word?' Grandma! First you want me to use my middle finger, and then you want me to think of the F-word?" We laughed, but I hoped he didn't tell his parents.

Sophia, Trent's half-sister and Alex's sister, was born on November 20, 2013. Pat and I had to wait until our seventies, but there was now a girl in the family! Sophia had bright red hair until about three years of age, when it started to tint more auburn. She is a bright, fun-loving princess, who at age five loves all the princess movies, jigsaw puzzles, playing house and dancing. Like Trent and Alex, she has brought us great joy and many memories, but one recent event will always remain with me.

On April 19, 2018, the anniversary of my sister RoseAnn's death, Justine, Sophia's mom, asked me if we could babysit Sophia for the afternoon while Adrianne, her regular day care provider, took her son to the doctor. In addition, we picked Alex up from school, and both Alex and Sophia were to be picked up around 5:00 when Brian got home from work. We had a fun time making cookies, doing jigsaw puzzles, blowing up balloons, etc. When Brian came, we were cleaning up and packing up when Sophia came into the kitchen and took my hand.

"Grandma," she said, "I have to show you something! Close your eyes!"

She held my hand as we made our way through the kitchen. "Keep your eyes closed, Grandma. It's a surprise." I couldn't imagine what she wanted to show me. I thought maybe she had put a puzzle together by herself or found an unusual bug. When we were near the front door, Sophia said, "Open your eyes, Grandma. See, there it is!" When I opened my eyes, and looked to where she was pointing, I saw on the steps going upstairs the reflection of refracted light coming from the narrow front door pane. The setting sun had created a rainbow on the carpet, and I felt immediately it was a gift from my sister RoseAnn. Sophia had led me in all innocence to it. Sophia would never know RoseAnn physically in her own lifetime, but somehow, I felt that Sophia's innocent spirit and my spirit as well were being nourished by the comforting, fleeting beauty of RoseAnn's touch. After that, I discovered that the light from the setting sun made differing reflections almost every day. We had lived in this house for over twenty years, and I had never noticed the beauty in the refracted rays. "Open your eyes, Grandma!"

In 2014, I joined a choral group that was just forming, directed by retired music teachers and welcoming college students, as well as older people who enjoyed singing. We gave concerts every year, but usually only Pat, my husband, attended. In 2018, however, we had what I considered a really good concert. So I invited my son Brian, his friend Mel, and Alex and Sophia to come. I wasn't sure if the children, then 8 and 4, would enjoy it, but I was eager for Alex to see a renowned symphony director who was accompanying us on the piano for Haydn's epic "Creation." After the concert, I asked Alex what he thought of the pianist, and his reply was unexpected but so much like Alex, "He was good, but I've seen better."

Two days later, Sophia and I were coloring together, and she said, "Grandma, you sang good the other night."

Me: "Oh, Sophia, thank you. Did you like the concert?"

Sophia: "Yeah, it was pretty good, but it was a little loud."

Me: "Oh was it too loud for you?"

Sophia: "Yeah, I couldn't fall asleep."

"Mama Needs a Hug"

My mother always tried to wring from misfortunes and tragedies some morsel, no matter how slight, to be thankful for: "Count your blessings" almost always came after something sad had happened. I think it was from her having faced such sorrows, and lost so many loved ones in her long life, that she grasped for ways not to let the sadness overwhelm her. Sometimes, it was a stretch. I remember when a young neighbor girl fell and broke her arm, and I was sadly relating the news to my mom, she said, "Well, it could be worse! Thank God she didn't fall on her head!" She always thought it was a blessing in disguise that I got to care for Trent when he was a young child, and over the years, I have begun to realize what a tremendous gift it was.

When Trent was seven, my mom died. I had been caring for her for a few weeks earlier, and Brian arrived on the morning she died with Justine, Trent, and Alex. They joined the family surrounding Mom's bed while her friend Herman from Meals on Wheels played his violin, and we all sang "Amazing Grace." Trent was quiet, but he seemed to understand that Great Grandma Knight had gone to heaven. Later that same summer, we went to South Dakota for a Carey family reunion and to celebrate Grandma Carey's 100th birthday. Trent had a great time, but at one point, he remarked, "What's so great about 100 years old? Great Grandma Knight was 104!"

When Trent was about three-and-a-half, and we played "Go Fish," he had a sensitivity to me that was really endearing. Even though he sometimes knew what cards I had, he never asked me for them. He didn't hesitate to ask Grandpa if he had a Sammy Shark, or Dexter Dolphin, or Walter Whale, but if he knew I had one that he needed, he would always ask me for something else.

Ever since he was a toddler, Trent loved to pick flowers and give them to me—mostly dandelions and wild flowers. When he brought them to me, we put them in a vase or added them to flowers that were already in the house. Sometimes while he was sitting on Grandpa's lap while mowing the lawn with Grandpa, he'd have Grandpa stop, and he'd jump off the lawnmower, pick a wild flower along the side of the yard, and run in the house to give it to me.

One time when he was five, we were going somewhere in the car when we saw some men working on a roof. Trent said that they had sticky stuff on their feet so they wouldn't fall. Then he thought again and said no, they didn't have sticky stuff. They were just walking at a "small bend," and it wasn't that hard. I said I wouldn't want to do it, and he said, "Grandma, when I get big, I'll take you by the hand and help you walk up on the roof, okay?" He also said, "Grandma, when I get big, and you need anything fixed, you just call me, and I'll come over and fix it right away."

I was giving Trent a ride home another day when he said out of the blue, "Grandma, I wish I were Grandpa." I was amazed that he used the subjunctive mood correctly at age five—he really had picked up good speech patterns! I asked him why he wished he were Grandpa, and he just said, "I just wish I were." I wondered if it was his Grandpa's teaching in college, the books he had written, his carpentry work, his golf game, etc., so to keep the conversation going, I asked, "What would be the best thing if you were Grandpa?" I will always treasure his innocent reply, "Then I could always be around you."

When Trent first started staying overnight with us at age three, he occasionally got homesick. He never said, "I want to go home" or anything else. He would always just sob, "Mama needs a hug! Mama needs a hug!"

One night after Grandpa put five-year-old Trent to

bed, Grandpa came downstairs and told me what Trent had said, "Grandpa, when you and Grandma are up with the angels, can I come and stay with you because I love you both so much."

Trent, we will be watching over you and all of our family with the angels and, God willing, after you have all had long, fulfilling lives on earth, we will be waiting for you with open arms.

Grandma and Grandpa need hugs!

Irish Shenanigans and Souvenirs

It doesn't seem possible that my husband and I have been married for fifty years as of December, 2022. After the wedding in 1972, we settled into a small apartment in the Bronx where Pat was working on his doctorate at Fordham University, and I got a job teaching high school English nearby in New Jersey. Because of the research and my job, we postponed our honeymoon until the summer of 1974 when we traveled to Ireland, the land of our heritage and our dreams.

We initially flew overnight to London, took a train to Liverpool and then boarded a ferry to Dublin. After some 30 hours of traveling, we were exhausted when we arrived in Dublin, and so we hailed a cab and asked the taxi driver to take us to the nearest hotel. Once there, we fell into bed. Holy Mother Machree—the bed collapsed! Welcome to Ireland! Sprawled on the floor, too tired to move, we slept on the caved-in mattress until morning.

We could have taken the crashed bed as an omen for things to come, but we found it too humorous to take seriously. Diarmaid Ferriter has written a book about the 70s in the Republic of Ireland: *Ambiguous Republic,*

Ireland in the 70's (2012). Although there were serious issues, conflicts, and crises, Ferriter also recognized the celebrations and triumph of Irish culture in this decade. We found Ireland on our honeymoon very much alive, welcoming, warm, and wonderfully musical,

Because we had little money, our itinerary for the most part consisted of hitchhiking from one point of interest to another and staying at Bed and Breakfasts and educational institutions while Pat did research for his dissertation. Though hitchhiking in a foreign country may seem dangerous to the reader, in the seventies in the Republic of Ireland, it was a common practice for people of meager means. We were young, healthy, and traveled lightly with backpacks. We also met some wonderful people in the process. One such encounter happened on a Sunday morning when we were hitchhiking on a country road with little traffic except an occasional herd of sheep. A small camper pulled up beside us on the road, and a priest appeared at the wheel. "Have you eaten your breakfast yet?" he called out. No, we hadn't. He pulled over and invited us into the back of his trailer. There he had a small table and stools. He was going home from saying Sunday Mass at a nearby village and hadn't yet had his breakfast. Before long, he had fixed us eggs, Irish bread, meat and a cup of tea with milk. We had a wonderful conversation, and as we thanked him and were about to leave, I asked him what kind of meat it was he had prepared as I had never had it before. "Why, sure, it's blood sausage," he said. I managed to get out of the trailer and say my goodbyes before I almost lost my breakfast. We soon learned, of course, that blood sausage, or "black pudding," is an Irish staple, but it was an early "culture shock" that I well remember.

Because the Irish speak English, it is so much easier to travel in Ireland than in countries where the language differs, but sometimes even English is a problem. One of the places we planned to stay at in Ireland was St. Patrick's College in Carlow. Pat knew of some valuable historical sources there, so he had arranged for us to stay at the college while he did his research. Because we would be there for awhile—and since cell phones weren't in use in the seventies—I gave the address to relatives and friends in case they needed to get in touch with us in the months while we were in Ireland.

We arrived at St. Patrick's mid-morning on a rainy week day. The nun who greeted us was very warm and welcoming. At one point, I asked her, "Do we by chance have any mail?" She looked at me a bit strangely, but then smiled and asked us to sit while she left the room. She seemed to be gone for quite a while but then returned and asked us to follow her. She led us into a room where a table was set with boiled ham, Irish bread, and fresh fruit. We gratefully ate the meal, but I soon learned that the Irish expression for "mail" is "post," and that the nun had mistaken my request for "mail" for a "meal." I was thoroughly embarrassed and apologized, but there, and all through our trip, we were amazed by the spontaneous hospitality of the Irish that we encountered everywhere.

And we encountered many other tourists in our travels in Ireland. One day we rented bicycles to take a ride around the Slea Head Loop on the Dingle Peninsula. It was a beautiful day, and the estimated three-hour ride afforded breathtaking views of the ocean and the Blasket Islands and the possibility of touring the ancient beehive huts and seeing an Iron Age fort. We thoroughly enjoyed the first half of the trip, and then we decided to stop for lunch at a pub where we could hear Irish music playing. When we were almost finished with lunch, two German tourists came in the pub. They walked over to our table, and one of them asked us with a bewildered look on his face and a strong German accent: "Are those your bicycles out there?" We said they were, and the German shook his head and looked at us just finishing our Guinnesses and sandwiches. "Don't you know," he said, "when you ride bikes and drink beer, your knees are going to turn to bricks!" No, we didn't know, but we soon found out. Needless to say, we learned a valuable lesson for the rest of the trip, but that day, we walked our bikes most of the way back to the bike rental.

In the seventies and eighties, Pat and I took my

mother, sister-in-law, and Pat's parents on different trips to Ireland: wonderful memories of driving the winding roads, eating hearty gourmet meals, and visiting villages where our families had their roots. Then in the nineties while I was teaching Irish Literature on the university level, I delivered a paper at a literary conference in Dublin. It was in the early 2000's, however, that I co-led two groups of university students (2005), (2009) and at another time a group of alumnae and friends (2006) to both the Republic of Ireland and Northern Ireland.

While the students studied Irish Literature, sociology, and women's leadership on the student trips, they and we as leaders were so enriched by the Irish and Northern Irish leaders we met along the way who spoke to our group. President Mary McAleese (1997-2007) greeted us each personally at *Áras an Uachtaráin* in Phoenix Park, Dublin. We had informative and insightful talks from Mary Coughlan, Minister for Agriculture (2004-2008); Joanna McMinn, Director of the National Women's Council of Ireland; Evelyn Conlon and Felicity McCall, Irish novelists and short story writers; Dan McCall, Department of Education, Northern Ireland; Tony Gallagher, Professor of Education, Queens' University, Belfast; Mairead Corrigan Maguire, Northern Ireland peace activist; and Monica McWilliams, co-founder of the Northern Irish Women's Coalition and participant in the Good Friday

Peace Agreement in Northern Ireland. Monica was instrumental in arranging for most of our speakers at the Women's Center in Belfast. She has recently published her memoir: *Stand Up Speak Out: My life working for women's rights, peace, and equality in Northern Ireland* (2021).

One of the most memorable talks we experienced was given by John Hume (1937-2020), one of the leaders in the Northern Ireland Peace Process, who was awarded the Nobel Peace Prize, the Gandhi Peace Prize, and the Martin Luther King Award. Following his talk, before he left, he sang "Danny Boy" for our group. To listen to a man who had devoted his life to promoting peaceful solutions to conflict was deeply moving, as was his singing of Danny Boy: "And I shall sleep in peace until you come to me."

Our groups explored the South and North of Ireland with tours of Dublin, Galway, and Sligo, with trips to Glendalough, the Ring of Kerry, the Aran Islands, the Cliffs of Moher, the Inishowan Peninsula and dinner at Bunratty Castle as well as tours of Belfast, Derry, the Giant's Causeway, Corrymeela and Downpatrick in the North. In Dublin, we saw plays at the Abbey Theater, and in Belfast, students and group leaders signed the Peace Wall and visited Parliament, where Gerry Adams, long time president of Sinn Féin, was sighted between sessions.

These trips to Ireland were educational, enjoyable and inspiring, and they also had their unintentional memorable aspects. One of those experiences was our first journey with students in 2005 when we chartered a bus from Dublin to Glendalough. We rode through the Wicklow Mountains over winding, bumpy roads and sharp curves on an extremely windy day. Some of the students began to feel queasy. We managed to make it to Glendalough without any major interruptions but about halfway on the way back, the bus driver got a call saying that we had unfortunately left a student at Glendalough (no doubt in the restroom). Somehow, our counting-attendance method had failed. What that meant, however, was going back over the winding, curvy, windy bumpy hills to pick up our lost one. Those who were already queasy became more so, and others joined them. Although the bus had a built-in restroom, on the return trip, the bus driver had to stop twice to let students out to relieve themselves of their breakfasts, lunches, snacks. Needless to say, the scent on the bus became nauseating in itself. It was a trip I doubt any of us will forget.

By the time we left Ireland on that first study trip there, some of the students put together a list of "Twenty-One Signs It's Time to Leave Ireland." Here are a few of them:

*When Dramamine becomes your new daily vitamin.

*When you consider Febreeze your new perfume.

*When you, yourself, start apologizing for Ireland's weather.

*When you know every article of clothing that every woman on this trip has in her bag.

*When wind blowing 80 miles per hour feels like a cool breeze.

*When some people in the group have begun to think they're Irish and have developed Irish accents.

*When you have the urge to clap for any statement that is made.

*When you start describing distances as a "five-minute walk."

*When you find yourself beginning to consider black pudding as an option.

In 2006 our trip to Ireland was unique because the President, Vice President of the university and I took a group of alumnae and friends with us on a cultural and sight-seeing tour of Ireland, both the North and the South. One of the friends who came with us was my oldest sister, JoAn, who had been to Ireland several times before but loved it as much as I did. Without students and syllabi, the ambiance on the trip was much different. Two of the alumnae created a custom of buying cookies, cakes, crackers and cheese at our various stops and serving snacks on the bus rides to our various destinations.

One morning in Dublin before the planned activities for the day, four of us, including JoAn, decided to go to Arbour Hill Cemetery where many of the heroes of the

1916 Irish Rebellion are buried. We arrived in time to view the daily raising of the colors and to hear the recorded national anthem of the Irish Republic.

We had just visited the grave of James Connolly, a leader of the Easter Rising in 1916 who was later executed for his role in that rebellion, when JoAn spotted a tree nearby that had an unusual growth at the top. As we walked toward it over the cement that was wet from the recent rains and dew, JoAn slipped and fell. As she fell, she tried to land in the nearby garden but instead ended up hitting her hip on the ridge of marble that lined the garden. The cemetery caretaker, who was working in the garden at the time, quickly came to our aid, went and brought a desk chair with wheels, and we transported JoAn to the United Nations Veterans Office in the cemetery. Although JoAn was in quite a bit of pain from the fall, the caretaker suggested an Irish remedy: He fixed her some hot tea and Paddy's Irish Whiskey, which seemed to ease the pain quite a bit.

We decided it would be well to go to the emergency room at the nearest hospital to be sure there were no internal injuries, so JoAn and I took a cab to St. James' Hospital. When JoAn told the nurse in the E.R. what had happened, the nurse said, "Ahh, you poor thing! You fell on your bum!" From then on the term became part of our vocabulary.

While we waited for the tests, JoAn began to feel a bit giddy (perhaps from the Paddy's but also perhaps from the codeine-based pain-killler the nurse gave her). She showed me the injury on her hip that was rapidly taking on a colorful shape, and the thought occurred to us that this "accident" might be a "blessing in disguise." Here we were in Ireland, land of druids, fairies, and sprites, and we had just experienced a mysterious apparition on JoAn's bum! With suitable draping we could take pictures and make replicas—key chains, balloons, coins, mugs, greeting cards—of the mystical image appearing in an Irish cemetery.

When all the tests were finished, the doctor told us the injury was a hematoma and that there was nothing to be done about it but to apply ice and take more pain killers (Paddy's? Jameson's??). When we shared the episode and our creative ideas for the image with the rest of our fellow travelers, they came up with many other insightful suggestions including "bum fund-raising" activities for charitable causes.

Our group stayed in touch after we left Ireland, and we planned a summer reunion at the university where I was teaching. There, JoAn gave an update of her injury with pictures and a written text:

As it turns out, the image on my bum went from a mysterious figure, to a map of Ireland, and then to a map of the United States. From there it began to fade away, and now there is no vestige of this former work of art. Plus, the hematoma that was buried deep inside has diminished to almost nothing. Apparently, I am healed! Lessons learned:

1. Being overweight has its positive side effects (and positive bum effects).
2. If you are going to fall down, fall down in Ireland where they know what to do when you fall down (e.g., tea and Paddy's).
3. If you are seriously injured, do not fall down in Ireland, because the emergency health care system (although friendly and competent) is backed up for hours (but you may be inspired to write poetry or sagas or create other works of art while you wait).
4. Fall down with your sister and friends nearby; moral support is everything.
5. Be aware that those around you constitute a walking pharmacy with medical equipment (pillows, ice packs, aspirin, etc.).
6. Don't ever let your sister see your bum!!!

In 2012, Pat and I returned to Ireland for ten days with our sons and a daughter-in-law for their first visit. We rented a house near Doolin and used that as a base to travel out to Killarney, Dingle, the Ring of Kerry, Cork, the Cliffs of Moher, Galway, and the Aran Islands. We finished the trip with a few days in Dublin. Our sons fell in love with Ireland as we had and have since traveled back on their own with their wives and families.

In October 2019, our older son, Brian, invited Pat and me to go with him, his wife, Mel, and their five children to Ireland for a week. They rented a guest house called "The Mill" in County Cork, and we used it as our base. The house was on Nohoval Cove, so we were able to spend many hours exploring the beach with the children, but we also took day trips to Blarney Castle where we watched the grandkids kiss the Blarney stone as we had done almost fifty years previously. We visited the Titanic Museum in Cobh and Fort Charles on another day. Brian wanted his kids to see the Cliffs of Moher, so we traveled one rainy, misty day to stand in the wind and see once again the magnificent cliffs. All in all, it was a wonderful trip, and sharing it with two younger generations was all the more enriching.

A minor but strange thing happened on this trip that has stayed with me and left me pondering. When we first arrived in Dublin, Ireland, and were loading our luggage into rental cars at the Dublin airport, I noticed not far from our car a chain lying on the rain-soaked cement. It was clearly part of a jewelry set, but since there was no way to find the owner, I took it with me as a surprise souvenir from Ireland. On our fourth night at the Mill House, we were going to a special dinner, so I dug through my suitcase for my Celtic necklace. I found the Celtic symbol, but the chain was missing. In an instant I realized that the chain I had found in the Dublin airport was my own. How it had detached itself from its pendant, which was fastened with a metal loop, and left the inside pocket of the suitcase, which had not been opened, I'll never understand, but being a scholar of Irish literature, I felt immediately that the episode, if inexplicable, must be symbolic.

At first, I thought about it personally. What chains was I carrying around with me that I needed to lose? Habits of thought that were tying me down? Needless worries? On the other hand, what links with others did I need to strengthen? What broken connections needed mending? But then, of course, I pondered the context: finding links I didn't even know were missing in a foreign land, in my ancestral home, at a time when the links in our own family line were present. Like the starting chain in a crochet pattern, I now see the chain as an image of all the connections in life, sometimes lost sight of, but linking us with the past, our heritage, the present in all its mystery, and the future promise. The Irish souvenir that I found at the airport, which was in one way mine to begin with, reminds me of our links with all others who have touched our lives and whose lives we have touched in the invisible patterns of our human existence. I hope the new-found vision of that mystical chain is never lost.

Acknowledgments

I am greatly indebted to many people throughout the years who have read portions of this collection and given suggestions. Although they may not realize it, Mary Beth Duffey and Kathleen Scullin have provided encouragement and renewed energy by reading some stories and giving me comments, and most importantly, by remembering the stories years later. In putting together the final collection, I am deeply indebted to my husband, Pat, for reading, enjoying, making suggestions, and encouraging me to publish. I greatly appreciate his love and support, especially as he is a much-published scholarly writer himself.

My sisters JoAn Knight Herren and Barbara Knight Johnson and my friends Patricia O'Donoghue and Catharine Malloy gave me honest and enthusiastic feedback on later drafts of the collection. Their invaluable suggestions greatly energized my revisions.

I also want to acknowledge Shannon Ishizaki from Ten16 Press for her always encouraging responses during the publication process and Kaitlyn Hein, for her excellent editing suggestions. Kaitlyn was extremely helpful in the final revisions. I am also grateful to Lauren Blue for her expertise in formatting the text and for her endless patience in making my minor changes and to Tom Heffron for his very creative and insightful designing.

My life experiences have been formed and enriched by family, friends, colleagues, students and sometimes complete strangers. My sincere gratitude to those who comprise these memoirs as well as to the many others whose lives have intertwined with mine. Lastly, I thank the readers who take the time to read this collection and who find in our shared memories the threads of our bonds with one another, the humor that lifts our spirits, and the patterns of meaning that shape our lives.

www.ingramcontent.com/pod-product-compliance
Lightning Source LLC
LaVergne TN
LVHW041216080426
835508LV00011B/976